He Speaks

"How lovely is your tabernacle, O LORD of hosts! My soul longs, yes even faints for the courts of the LORD; My heart and my flesh cry out for the living God."
Ps. 84:1-2

>Thank you for walking with me when I am weak. Thank you for being my friend and lifting me up. Show your glory Lord. Reveal your heart to this generation- teach them your love and that you alone are Truth. Bring them to new places in their walk with you. Strengthen and encourage but also edify and sanctify their belief. My trust is in you Lord, for you alone ARE GOD.

BE EXCITED. Jesus Christ is alive. He has called you to this place to reveal His love for you. Know He is here in this moment and is FOR YOU. He is mighty to save.

He Speaks by Nicole Bishop
Published by Lulu.com
Lulu Press, Inc.
3101 Hillsborough Street
Raleigh, NC 27607
www.lulu.com

This book or parts thereof may not be reproduced in any form, stored in a retrieval system, or transmitted in any form by any means-electronic, mechanical, photocopy, recording or otherwise – without prior written permission of the publisher, except as provided by United States of America copyright law.

Unless otherwise noted, all Scripture quotations are taken from The Nelson Study Bible New King James Version, copyright © 1979, 1980,1982 by Thomas Nelson, Inc.

International Standard Book Number:
978-1-329-85946-3

DEDICATION

I dedicate this book to my daughter, Briana. I pray that these words Jesus spoke to me in this journal will come alive for each one of you as they did for me. I pray that this book would be a springboard for your walk with Jesus, that you develop an even deeper relationship with Him through Scripture and conversations.

ACKNOWLEDGMENTS

I want to give thanks to my two Holly's in my life. I would not be where I am in my walk if it were not for these two women of God. Holly Simmons, for her fearless spirit and endurance to study God's Word. A woman, who walked along side of me early in my walk, mentored me and inspired me.

Thanks to Holly Avera, for believing in me, encouraging me and being there for me when I am scared to step out in faith. I am thankful for her peace of God she carries with her everywhere she goes. Her love of the Lord radiates from her and is a blessing to all those who know her. Thank you for writing the Forward.
I want to give special thanks to my husband, Gus for his leadership and love he has given to our family and me. His unbridled faith and uncompromising efforts to seek the Lord and have others seek Him inspires me. To my Son, Bailey who has the heart of Jesus for the least and the lost. To my Daughter, Briana who loves others like Jesus calls us to love. I love you Lord, thank you for calling me friend.

FOREWARD

It's been a pretty normal day so far. You come home from work or school. You go in your room, turn on some music, maybe grab the iPad and open Netflix, ready to occupy your mind for a little, or get ready to go for a run to clear your head, or maybe change clothes real quick before going to meet some friends to study at Starbucks.

You've been a little off lately. You can't put your finger on it. You just know some things aren't making sense. Something is going on inside. In your head. In your heart. Somewhere inside. But you don't want to think about that right now. And then there's a knock on your door. You pause. You must have heard wrong or thought you heard it. Another knock. You're sure you heard it this time. You go to the door and open it. And there he is. This guy. You know him. You can't quite place where but you know that you know him. He says "Hi" and smiles, and everything is different, because you now feel more alive and more you than you've ever felt before.

And all he said was "hi." And he has so much more to say...

Nicole heard a knock, opened the door, and when He began to speak, she pulled up a chair, got comfy, and listened. What you're about to read is their conversation. Her questions, His answers. Her responses. His prayers. Maybe you'll sit down and read it in one sitting. Maybe you'll read a little at a time. But the pace is not the point, the conversation is. And once you are reading theirs, you can't help but begin you're own.

This book is an invitation. Not a general invite sent in the mail to "current resident" or sent to your email that immediately is marked as spam or like a note your parent left for you "inviting you to do your chores"-we know that's not an invite, but a "do you chores or consequences will follow." This invitation is in person. Its real. This is hearing the sound of His voice, seeing His posture and soft smile,
looking into His eyes filled with hope. Hope that we will choose. Hope that we will receive. Hope that we will listen to all He wants to say, because as Nicole makes it clear, He speaks.

He speaks and teaches us now to speak: not with volume but with gentleness. A gentleness so powerful it changes lives forever. To speak not with intimidation but with authority. Authority that was given to you to build up others. Authority that does not demand others to their knees before ourselves, but invites others to join us on our knees before Him.

You're invited!

There's a knock at the door...

5

INTRODUCTION

Daughter of The King,

I am so excited to share what The Lord spoke to me about you. In the Summer of 2015 on Panama City Beach, The Lord placed on my heart the desire to write a quiet time journal for all His daughters. In reverence and trembling, I sat on the beach with my journal waiting for Him to speak. This book is what He spoke to me for you. This book is His desire for you to know Him like never before. He IS love. He desires you to spend time with Him, get to know Him – not only as Savior but also as friend.

- The regular font is me speaking to Him, praying and asking Him questions.
- What He spoke to me is italicized and in quotations.
- The scripture is in bold.
- The italicized quotations after scripture are His commentary about what He just asked you to read in scripture.
- The open spaces are meant for you to journal back to Him.

This book changed my life. I have never been closer to Jesus than I am now. My heart's desire is for you to know Him and seek His face and hear His voice, because He Speaks.

I am thankful for you Lord in all your ways, speak to those who yearn to know you.

"To all those here reading My words, know I have chosen her to speak these truths. She loves Me with a pure heart and yearns desperately for you to know Me more.

To those who's valley is deep, be aware your trouble will come to an end. Though your persecution comes from all sides, My strength is in you. Stand up, call upon My Name and exalt Me in their presence and watch the enemy flee.

For those not feeling strong enough or bright enough, take My wings and fly. My power is in you through My Spirit. Lift your wings and feel Me in the breeze. Things will move and shift beneath you but trust in My guidance and know that I AM your loving Father.

For those who don't know Me, I AM real. I put breath in your lungs and watch you move around day-to-day weak in your flesh searching for more. It's Me your soul longs for, its Me that satisfies.

Take my hand and give me a chance. I will make all things new. I AM not like earthly fathers with weak flesh. **I AM.** *There is power in My Name. Call upon it and ask to see My attributes, ask to trust in Me and reveal My ways. I AM here with My hand stretched out waiting until YOU are ready. Come close, I AM good.*

For those who feel lost and abandoned, trust in Me. I have never left you despite your enemies and their efforts to destroy you. Come close to Me and let Me in to your secret place. My love for you is pure and I want you to have life in abundance and soar. Though the seas get rough and the waves crash along your vessel – I AM stronger. Call upon Me to calm your storm."

"This is the dawn of a new day for you and Me. Its light is dim but I AM near. You fear the waves, but I hold them back. Trust in My strength and rely on Me. I know you feel like you are having to settle. Like this is all there is and this little crumb will have to do. I have abundance planned for you. Be overjoyed in expecting My goodness and favor."

Its scary Lord. How can I be excited when things always go back to chaos- life distracting me from you?

"Be Strong. Be intentional about your time with Me, pray for favor with your schedule and spend time with Me first each day."

"My Word renews and brings life to the broken and betrayed. My Word is hope and love. My spirit indwells every page. Call upon Me to give you truth and explain its inner meanings. The enemy deceives and makes those feel bored or un-inspired. Pursue Me. Draw near to Me and love My Word. Devour its pages like a king's banquet. My Words satisfy the inner parts of you that nothing else reaches."

"How do you know me? As an angry dictator or loving dad? Do you hear of Me from others but are scared to let Me in? Hear my voice crying out in the wilderness of your heart."

Read Song of Songs. *"I AM the He and you are the she. Read these verses as My yearning to draw you to Me. Though it is written as lovers it's your pure beauty I see. Love yourself and see yourself as I see you.*

Do not let the perversion of what some men have done to love influence you from knowing My love.

How I love you and yet you still fear me. Take My hand and walk with Me."

Haggai *"Read these words and know the things of this world fade and wither. Work done through Me endures. The enemy's snare is to call you to little. Believe in Me. My things I call you to are huge, vast and without bounds. Re-build My house in you. Fortify your walls and prevent the enemy from distracting you from your calling."*

Haggai 2:4b *"I AM with you. I have called you to this place. I see you and I see where I have planted you and you are not a mistake. Although things seem out of place and discouraging at times, these things strengthen you. Don't feel like you have gone too far and cannot come back to Me. I AM here and we are together. Let's see what work can be done in this place together.*

My signet ring is proof you are working for Me. I have given you authority in this place to speak for Me to those who won't listen. Speak in a gentle voice – call upon My spirit to loosen their chains and break down their walls. The workers are few. You are here, reading this because you are one of My workers with a heart for the lost. Stand firm in your faith and love My people. Teach them My ways. Don't let your flesh of rejection or worry distract you from your calling. Open your eyes and search for their hurting. I AM preparing the way."

"Those who feed others, I cause people to gather. Although it might seem weird and that they are capable of feeding themselves-they are young in their faith and need your fruit."

"Where will you go to tell people about Me? Where is Holy Spirit guiding you? Be strong and don't fear. I have already gone before you and prepared the way."

Luke. *"My gifted writer, follower of truth. Read these passages and know My background and My works while here in the flesh. Consider your role in this book for this age."*

Holy Spirit –open their eyes – change them as a column of fire of passion for you-Amen.

"Just like Zechariah you feel randomly chosen and just going through the motions. Like you are not quite sure you are in the right place. Although Zechariah was chosen by "lot" his place in My temple was not an accident and neither is your place- I see your desires and AM listening. When its time, new things will birth."

"I will find you in your workplace and show My love. You will begin to change those around you in a kinder way. Although you feel like you might have missed your calling, you have not. Your mission field is here and now where you are. Stop and look around. Want to know Me more. Reach deep inside and speak truths to them on My behalf. Seek My wisdom in your words and don't fear rejection —it's only your flesh making you weak."

Lord, your beauty amazes me. Your splendor in your creation causes me to cry. Teach me about your colors and beauty of heaven.

"The colors are of Zion- a new shade of colors too magnificent to behold with your current eyes. The peace surrounds and fills you with full and complete love with nothing lacking. All here love and all here sing My songs. Rejoice your loved ones are here. Seek Me and join them one day. My heart for all My children is to just take My hand and trust Me. WALK in love. Walk out your faith journey now. Preach boldly in the streets and homes. Proclaim My love. Don't condemn those who are alone and don't know of Me. Those, I yearn for most. My eye is on the least and those who feel all hope is lost."

Thank you for the life you give. Thank you for being a loving Father who gently ignores our stomping foot wanting things our way right now.

Luke 6:44-45
Use me Lord to speak life and truth into those around me. Hear my cry to reach the lost, bind in me what is not of you. Loosen the things you have placed in my heart. Reveal to me YOUR ways. – Amen

Luke 8:15 *"Times are tough and cause you to reveal your faith or lack there of. The tough times I have orchestrated because you need to grow in those areas. Do not flee in fear but boldly proclaim MY strength to conquer pain and fearful circumstances. My strength is in you. You are NOT weak. It is time to call the enemy a liar and leave him by the wayside- no longer able to affect you or your strength."*

Luke 8:25 *"All things are in My control, the Word is powerful and My NAME is strong. Speak boldly in MY Name; claim victory in MY name and it will be done. Don't fear My power when you see it at work. Share it so others will be built up and want to use it too. Believe in the resurrection power. I AM alive and I rose again. Having faith in Me you will too. Call to life the things that seem dead. They are merely sleeping in you."*

Luke 8:40-56
Lord, what are we lacking faith to believe you can heal and resurrect? It seems like only your resurrection power was displayed during biblical times.

"My power is in all who believe. Resurrection is from My Father who wills it. There are many hurts and wounds that need to be repaired by faith. If you dare to touch my garment in your faith you will be healed. Although My physical garment no longer remains with you, My heart is with you. Reach out your hand and surrender your hurt, your brokenness and sickness. Your faith in Me is what heals you."

Luke 9:20 *"Am I the Christ in your life or are you living in your strength, believing only good things come from hard work and determination? I watch you work and toil, hard work is well but there are many burdens you keep that I can release. Remove these burdens and I will multiply your efforts 10 fold. Faith in Me has much power. It heals, resurrects and replenishes. Seek Me instead of earthly solutions."*

Lord, I want to resurrect my trust. My trust that being vulnerable to people here on this earth won't hurt me. I keep them away at a safe distance and walk a guarded life.

"People will let you down, but much happiness comes from being vulnerable. I guard in you what matters and protect you in My love. Their hurt they cause is fleeting and only lasting a moment in time. It comes from their weakness that they lash out in revenge, anger and rejection. It is not personal its their lack of relationship with Me, stay close to them and pray for them and these lonely people will know My love. If someone is causing you physical harm, or emotional harm, flee from them, they are not of Me."

Lord, strengthen me like the mighty oaks at Mamare. Help me to see myself as the strong oak you have made me. Help me reject the thought of weakness, insignificance, and irrelevance. Help me to only seek approval from you and not yearn for attention and approval from man. In Jesus name, Amen.

"Don't be afraid to shed the things that are causing you harm and draining the life out of you. Drop them and I will bring forth new life from old wood. Although you feel weak and overcome, don't fear, I see the life and abundance in you. Although you feel like you've been wandering around and just "ended up" here, you are right where I have called you to be. Remove regrets from decisions in your past and forgive yourself. I don't see you as someone who has failed, but someone who perseveres. Love yourself, you have not missed out on My blessings because of your past, there are many blessings yet to be revealed."

Give me eyes to see the future, to be excited for the things you see to be revealed. I want to run, hope and love without fear.

"There are many things you see that you don't like, they tie you down and burden you, I have made a way to remove those. Be excited in My strength and things will be made new. Heavy burdens and despair are not of Me. Bind those lies and believe in Me. Give Me your burdens and they will flee."

"Those of you who are yearning to be close but you have yet to reveal your heart to Me. Although I see your inner heart, it does you no good if you don't willingly show it to Me. Admit your desires, your sins and your fears. Pride also blocks Me from you. Your pride is so strong you are blinded by it. Humility is where I flourish in you."

Luke 9:51-55 *"So quick to anger against those who are not like you or who reject you. That's the best place to reveal My love-when they are least expecting it."*

Luke 10:17 Why was it that time and time again the demons knew who Jesus was and submitted to Him, even the 72 who went out in your name but the leaders of the law- Pharisees and Sadducees, and some Jews today still can't see you?

"They are so caught up in traditions and the pride of their ways rather than listening to The Father. Their pride comes from their heredity of man; not found in Me- pride of tradition, protocol, procedure and perfection. I require none of these. A willing heart to hear My voice and My Father's love is all I need."

What about the demons-how do they know? *"They were created angels who became prideful. Not humans with My breath in them."*

Luke 10:41 *"Worry and anxiety come from failing in the past. Failure is not as bad as you fear. Your strength grows as you have courage to try new things. Perfection is a form of pride. Go out in love, ask for My strength and will to be done and anxiety will be overcome."*
"People see Me to be seen and only to get a glimpse of Me. My glory that comes from the Father is fully revealed to those who get up early, seek refuge or stay up late to find Me."

Luke 11:21
Why did he fall and loose his possessions?
"He was guarding his own house in his own strength. Strength comes from any other source but Mine is weak. It's a lie many believe."

Luke 11:44 *"Honor from man leads to death. It draws Me away from you because you are seeking glory."*

Luke 11:52 *"Going through the motions and coming up feeling empty feels that way because it is empty. How beautiful is your cup, but it does you no good to walk around with it empty and without Me."*

Luke 12:11 *"The Holy Spirit is in this author and has asked to reveal My heart to you. These pages are life and anyone can hear from Me, just as she does. Her heart cried out in desperation for the Holy Spirit to teach her My Word and it was granted to her by faith. Come to Me with the same vulnerability and faith and things will be revealed to you whenever you ask."*

Luke 12:31 *"I have provided for you all the things you have asked for and more. You live in fear because you are trying to control when and if you will get whatever your heart desires. Do not live on the edge, not knowing if you will have enough, but don't live in strife to receive the excess."*

Luke 13:5 *"Life without repentance leads to death. Life without repentance leads to brokenness and worry. When you are full of sin you have not repented for, I am unable to get in and wash your heart clean."*

Luke 13:25 *"Do not be fooled by rituals created by man. They are but a beautiful vessel. If you walk around carrying or protecting an empty vessel it is of no use. Your vessel must be filled with Me to be made whole."*

Luke 14:11 *"Many fall in their quest to be honored. Insecure because they are wanting approval from man. My Father is the only one who can exalt without the fear of loosing their status."*

Luke 14:23 *"Many will hear My Name and think they have time or dismiss it as though useless. Pray for their heart, mind and BE love to them. Only love opens the eyes of the blind."*

"Do not feel inferior to those with eloquent speech. If I needed your task to be eloquent I would have given you that gift. Prayer and love is what opens and frees hearts, not correct speeches or rebuttals."

Luke 15:3-7 *"I see the single, the lost and alone. My heart breaks for those outside My love. Pray for eyes to see them and for words of love to express to them. They will know My Father's voice if you share it."*

Luke 15:11-24 *"The lost son is the one who lives in wealth and relies on things of this world to give him joy. When moths, rust and famine cause him to need Me I gladly open My arms to receive him. He does not deserve it-no one does. My death on the cross paid for all to <u>freely</u> enter the Kingdom if they repent and come to Me."*

Luke 15:25-32 *"Jealousy of others and envy is not of Me. It is deception by the enemy. Pride of "doing and being" blinded him from rejoicing for his brother."*

Luke 16:15 *"Why do you build up store houses here as though they will make a difference? It shows your lack of trust in My provisions. Peace from excess is false. I will always provide for you when you are wise with the provisions already given. Excess and the love of excess is false peace. Save what you will need but don't worry about failure because your excess is not the same as your brothers' excess. Your work to save the excess takes toiling-I can cause the same result with merely a thought. Ask Me to provide for you and trust in Me to be your comfort and security. That is where true peace and joy comes from."*

Luke 17:4 *"Hate and bitterness might feel warranted but it's not of Me and I cannot reside in a heart full of evil thoughts, desires and bitterness. Your hate for how they made you feel does not justify your feelings-its merely a deception the enemy uses and a form of pride. You feel justified in your anger as though it's a punishment you bestow on your enemy. Your enemy has the upper hand because he has allowed the enemy to fill you with pride. I alone am allowed to judge. Their weakness causes them to react and respond out of ways that are not of Me. Just as a mother bird feeds her sparrows until they are grown, you must realize that although people are in a full-grown body, they still must mature in Me. Forgive and feed them from your inner strength, which comes from Me. Cut the ties of the enemy that bind your walk with Me. Forgive those who have hurt you. I see your pain and all that was lost and will repay you all that you lost 10 fold."*

Luke 17:17-19 *"I see your heart for the lost and I am working. Continue to pray for them I AM with you when you speak. Although they are considered foreigners and outcasts by the Pharisees of today-My heart sees no variance between people. I see their hearts. Have faith, pray in My name, ask and it shall be given to you. Don't fear My power it is alive in you."*

Luke 17:26-37 *"True work is through My Father. If your relationship with Me and Him is your most prized possession then there is no fear of things to come. You have more riches than Solomon and his splendor. Focus on Me and My Father's will. Share My love through words of faith and acts of kindness."*

Luke 18:9-14 *"Whenever you go out seeking praise it will be muted. Seek Me and My kingdom for My glory and your reward will be great."*

Luke 18:16-17 *"A child is trusting of his parent and will follow because he knows he is loved."*

Luke 18:23 *"The rich man didn't realize that all his wealth came from God and if he gave it all up it would have been returned 100 fold. People's efforts here on earth are a false security."*

Luke 18:27 *"Why do you pray for the crumbs of things you desire-as though its honorable? Be bold and ask for your hearts desires-I know them anyway. When you withhold as though its honorable its really prideful because you lack the faith to believe I can do exceedingly more abundant things that you even desire. Ask Me knowing that in all your efforts that you could never achieve them and through Me they will become real. Trust in Me and dare to ask."*

Luke 18:34 *"Things are hidden until it is God's timing to reveal them. Don't be afraid to trust His timing. His timing has the best outcome. Needing to know the timing is lack of faith."*

Luke 18:35-42 *"The difference between the beggar and the others who passed by and rebuked him was his abandonment of pride. He had nothing to loose, he sought Me without fearing what others thought. So many passers by want to appear in control but they are merely pillars of sand. One strong push and they are in a heap. Their fear of God's control keeps them from receiving His power. The sight that was restored was a demonstration to those people that nothing is impossible through Me, but your faith must be willing."*

Lord help us see you. Help us not run when we find you. Help us to trust in you for you are the only <u>good</u> in this world. -Amen.

Luke 19:1-10 *"Zacchaeus had an expectant heart, he yearned to see Me and was quick to repentance. Many go through their whole lives not attempting either. There are some reading thinking you are too far gone. You have sinned too much   no such thing. All sins are the same in My eyes. Repent and give Me your best. A willing and repentant heart changes futures, and trust in Me changes lives. Your best is not possessions or wealth, your best is eagerness and willingness to let Me in your secret fears and hopes to make them new or make them come alive. I spoke breath into your nostrils; dreams are seeds I placed in your thoughts. If you trust Me to guide you the effort will be less burden on you. Not all dreams will come true, not everything you seek is best. But there are things you don't have because you have not dared to ask."*

Luke 19:11-27 *"Effort is multiplied 10x when done with the correct heart. Many work for their sake on the side of a ditch without viewing how ridiculous it looks. They toil, walk around strutting and puffed up as though their life's work made a difference, working to be noticed by men as "great." People are consumed with their selves and couldn't care less about the man in the ditch and the riches his work built. It's meaningless and a lie that is so often believed."*

What is right? How should we live? Why are we so easily deceived into thinking our hard work, achieving goals and wealth is what's best?

"Most men focus on attaining things instead of seeking My face. Anything worked out of greed is always a deception. Even if you attain all the wealth in the world, there's still emptiness because <u>things</u> don't satisfy. Only I can satisfy. It's not about how much you have or who admires what you have, its your inner joy that come from Me that others want. Some will seek it and some will see what's required and say it's too much because they want the tangible things of now versus the things that are eternal. Its like a child in a high chair- face all messy and kicking its feet- wanting more, just wanting to be fed through someone else's labor and not realizing how gluttonous they are. Kicking and screaming in their selfish want while those with little who seek Me and My will always have enough. Enough is enough. This world says you need excess. Enough IS ENOUGH. Be wise with what you have and prepare for the storms that come, but don't waste this life building excess to the point it enslaves you to work."

Luke 19:28-44 *"They gave Me their best- I asked and they responded. They even gave their coats for Me to trample with the colt's hooves. A willing heart to give to Me is very rare. Pride blinds any who have missed Me."*

Lord let us be the living stones that cry out to those working and not seeing you- open their eyes Lord-let us share your truth and grace.

Luke 19:45-48 *"Just because you are in the temple or temple courts doesn't make you a believer. A believer trusts in Me and doesn't seek gain or honor under the deception of My work. Their work is for material possessions; My work is for My Father. His house is holy, don't fool yourself into making it less."*

Luke 20:1-8 *"Wanting to be right is rooted in pride. They wanted to be right so much they missed out on Me. Deception of the enemy comes in all forms. Even those held in great honor can be deceived if they are relying on their own efforts and refusing to be wrong. Its how they appear that's blinding them-how others view them is their stumbling block."*

Luke 20:9-19 *"Many have come in My name and share My love and truth but many are beaten, ignored and rebuked. Pray for the hearts of the deceived. Pray their souls would want to know Me more."*

Luke 20:20-26 *"People get confused because they believe God can be fooled or mislead. Actions reveal the heart of man. Those who seek fame for themselves will eventually fall, but those who seek to glorify Me will have the greatest riches....walking with Me and having all things revealed by My side."*

Luke 21:1-24 *"Judgment must come, the time is near. Take hold and stand firm. Persecution comes in many forms. Others may be tormented by the rebuking of some. Be a voice crying out in the wilderness to those that will listen. Pray for words that speak life and open eyes."*

What is it about our rebellious nature that resists your truth and complete submission to you?

"Pride causes man to have a false sense of control. You move things around and go places merely to satisfy your needs. Control is a fallacy. I will let you go as far from Me as you want to go. I will let you control what you want to control. But anything that is not of Me or from Me will fall short and leave you empty and alone. I AM true comfort and wealth. Me alone. Let go. Trust, I Am the GOOD Father. The desires of your heart came from Me-I gave them to you, don't fear I will take them from you if you let Me lead. Troubles are like waves, some are big and some are small, if you obsess on them they cause fear and depression. Watch one come into the shore. It looks like it will consume you, but by the time it hits the beach it is but a mere wash. Know I see all your troubles and things to come. I control the wind and the waves. Allow Me to speak to them and calm your storms within."

Why should we submit to you Lord? Help those who are reading trust in you- that you are good and that giving over control is best.

"My motives are all that is pure. Only goodness flows form Me. Absolute peace and freedom originate in My Name. Pride causes people to resist Me. Wanting to control things in your timing is accepting less. Why settle for a grain of sand when I offer the shores? Why choose one star to view when I can show you endless galaxies? The true issue is knowing Me and My character. My character is found in the Bible and how page after page speaks My truth and My endless pursuit of man. Read the pages of the Old Testament and see how I did exactly as I said I would do. My character never changes. All things written will be fulfilled. Read how Jacob was faithful to give away his best but the was not required to. It's being willing to loose all things of this world and take up your cross and follow Me- that I am looking for. There are many levels of obedience, the deeper you go- the closer you will become, but more will also be required. There are many very early in their faith and are too weak to feed themselves. Be patient, you too were young in your walk once."

Luke 22:1-6 *"Many will betray Me in My Name. I am aware and it won't change the outcome. Steer away from those claiming My Name for gain. If they are not edifying My Father's Name for the Kingdom of God they are not of Me. Many are deceived and have a false faith in Me- that I am a mere creation. I created all things through My spoken Word-power given to Me by My Father. There is power in My Name. Use it when you fear."*

Luke 22:7-46 *"You fear things to the point of exhaustion because you haven't given them to Me. If you would know and trust that ALL things are for My glory you wouldn't have anything to fear. Pray that your faith would be strengthened and that your trust would be without bounds."*

Luke 22:47-48 *"Nothing gets by Me. Many come in a false way and try to approach the Father but will be turned away because their faith is but an act trying to impress people of this world."*

Luke 22:49-53 *"Darkness has its time to try and consume people. But that time is limited. Pray that you would be the light and reveal the path of those who have gone astray by the betrayer. Ask for Holy Spirit to speak life. Don't listen to the enemy try to provoke you to fear, anxiety, pressuring someone to decide in the moment. You are in My plan for My revelation. Freedom is in MY name. No Word spoken from My Father falls on void soil. Pray for softened hearts to let us in."*

Luke 22:54-62 *"There will be times you will deny Me. My love for you will not change. I love you."*

Luke 22:63-71 *"The Word came from My lips and was written down by My prophets and scribes. All things are working to achieve My Father's will. Those who believe in Me-much will be required, but much reward comes from an obedient heart."*

Luke 23:1-25 *"Although the people got their way, it was My Father's will. People resisted Me, tortured Me and crucified Me. I knew this day would come but it didn't make it any less heart breaking. People's hearts are full of impure thoughts and devotions. Although this was painful, it was done for the final sacrifice. I gladly followed My Father's will in this. People still crucify and deny Me now. They use Me for their gain or ignore Me until they need things granted to them in this life. I freely give to all that ask, but love doesn't want things, love comes from the Father and is complete in Him."*

How do we love the way you love?
"Don't look through the lenses of things to be obtained or status to be gained. Every person is in need of love. Although they might reject it because their external heart is hardened-everyone wants genuine love and honor. Don't honor sin and sinful choices, but honor them as My son or daughter-even if they have gone astray-I still see them and seek them."

Luke 23:26-43 *"Although the criminal had done bad deeds, he didn't exalt himself. He was aware of his actions and admitted them and was willing to face his consequences. He saw Me as Truth and called out to save him and it was so. Many will die in their sin for lack of faith and being blinded by pride."*

Luke 23:44-55

Luke 24:1-31 *"Eyes will be opened and I will be revealed to willing hearts. Teachers teach. Be ready for My Words when they come. Boldly proclaim My truth- people need strength grounded in truth."*

Luke 24:32-53 *"All things written by My prophets must come true. The evidence is the power within you when you let Me in."*

What do you want us to do/know?
"My power, My might, My Father's will. Focus on My Words and see waves as insignificant because they are. In your moment of fear and confusion give Me your circumstance and troubles to Me in faith and let go. Freedom is being unbound in your life because of your faith. Stretch beyond your comfort zone and see that I AM there too. I love you- rejoice. Many have longed to hear My Words but wouldn't allow them in. Faith opens the eyes of the blind, ears of the deaf, and the lame will walk. You are strong. I AM with you- persevere in My love. Love those who are lost. Be gentle in spirit and do not worry- I AM with you."

Psalm 21:1-13 Thank you Jesus for loving us and talking to mere dust. Your love and thoughtfulness in the smallest details amazes me

Romans 12:1-2 *"Renew your mind daily. The enemy crowds out My light and you must discern what is Truth. Renew it daily and speak My Truth over your life. I am good and good things come from Me. Do not fear evil, I have overcome it."*

I feel like I need to be doing something to protect myself, family, friends…prepare or I will miss it or mess it up.

"Prayer for those who are far from Me. Prayer for those who are in need. Prayer for the minds of the weak and strong. I know the hearts, but the flesh becomes weak. Build up your strength through obedience. Strength is not from doing, but being in My presence. Picture a huge father figure guarding your back and walking with you ready to offer you direction and advice. You are not weak when you rely on Me."

Hebrews 11:1-3 *"I cause things to come into existence. Just because it doesn't exist now doesn't meant it can't happen. Seek and ask for the impossible. All things are possible for those with enough faith to ask."*

Hebrews 11:4-16 *"The past bondage holds you back. You have moved from that place, but look back in fear because its what you know- the entirety. Where you are going is new, don't let the unknown frighten you- I'm leading you this time. There is a harvest and you are My worker. Stay and remain where I brought you. Feed My sheep they need courage and strength."*

Hebrews 11:17-19 *"Abraham was faithful even to give up what he thought was the miracle I gave him. Keep your blessings in an outstretched arm and open hand like a seed for others to come and feed."*

What does that mean?

"My blessings are not limited, you don't have to clutch them so tightly to your chest away from everyone. Hold them out for others to be blessed by them too. Share your faith and your wealth of wisdom that comes from Me."

36

John 9:1-12 *"Things are hidden to reveal My purpose. The wisdom of man is far more limited than mine. If you look to man for honor you will get discouraged, but if you seek to honor My Father who sent you, your reward will be great. Your weaknesses are not flaws. They are your markers that people identify with in you. No one wants to feel like they can never measure up- they need someone who also struggles and is willing to admit their weaknesses."*

"You have planted many things that people can rest and feed upon. Don't be deceived by the shows and displays of others. Many people fear My Word because of its strength. My strength and power comes from truth. Don't fear My control in your life. I offer life to the fullest and full of abundance. I know the plans I have made for you, they are not out of your reach. You are seeking Me and walking in My ways. Uproot things that distract, hear My small still voice that is rest."

John 11:1-7 *"I see those who pour themselves out for Me and are willing to mourn for the lost and dead inside. Don't fear that it seems like I'm not listening or coming right away. I know your heart and hurt for them and they are not dead. I'm coming- know that I hear your plea and I am coming. Their life won't end in eternal death."*

John 11:8-16 *"My strength is revealed in those who wait. You don't need to be in a rush. I know your hearts' desires; I won't let you miss the blessings in store for you - because you seek to help save the lost. I will not allow others to diminish you. I'm behind you and they can see Me guarding you."*

Joshua 11 *"Line up your enemies you battle in your mind. Line them up-those are your kings you fear- I will defeat them."*

King of Insecurity: I am never enough.

King of worry and anxiety: If I let my guard down something bad will happen.

King of fear of failure: If I go 100% and I fail, I will feel stupid for not seeing it before I fail.

King of depression:

King of intimidation:

King of:

"I The Lord am your God- we are dethroning these false gods/rulers over your life as of now."

"I Am Truth and this is the Truth that defeats these liars:

Adonai- King of Kings Lord of lords says:

To the king of insecurity: False idol, you have no authority here. I made you and you are enough. You are willing and capable to learn anything you don't already know.

To the king of worry and anxiety: False idol, you have no authority here. Your life is in My hands. Anything that happens will not overcome you. Your strength comes from Me.

To the king of fear of failure: False idol, you have no authority here. Don't defeat yourself in your mind before you start. Plan it out and push. Don't let a little set back cause you to feel the entire thing is failing. Just adjust your plan.

To the king of depression: false idol, you have no authority here. You are my daughter with a heart full of love. You love Me and love others at the deepest level. You love those that persecute you and hurt you. You have done great things with your life. This is a new chapter-new supplies and a fresh start- a re-boot for a productive and fruitful future. Don't let the standards of men define your success. Money is not wealth. Things will always be there, as you need them. Focus on Me and loving others. Enjoy the moments of life and live.

To the king of intimidation. You are like a cardboard cutout. You stand tall, as though you are strong and in charge, but actually you have no depth. When I look at you from other angles I can see you are fake."

In Jesus name I claim victory over these lies. They have been trampled by Truth. From this day forward I will see them for what they once were-knowing they are failures and are mere dust.

Numbers 14 *"Despite My signs and wonders displayed on earth-spoken through creation, revealing My power just by My voice, people have a rebellious heart towards Me. People who can see Me and hear from Me are telling you the place I am taking you is good. In your presumptions you choose to rule your own life as though you know best. I will allow you to wonder if that's your will to disobey Me and ignore My plea to hear Me. I Am life in abundance. It's your choice to see through the eyes of faith."*

John 12:1-11 *"Many want fame and glory for themselves and portray they know Me. It is a façade. They are mere puppets to suit their cause. If they idolize themselves it makes them feel worthy. Although I spoke the world into existence, I was merely doing the work of My Father. It was never intended for My glory, that's why I fled large crowds. People are so easily swayed when it comes to serving their needs. Watch them- are they seeking fame for themselves or My Father's kingdom? I didn't create you to be a puppet- I gave you breath, skills and talents to honor My Father. When you fear man and follow the patterns of this world and what it values, you become a mere puppet. Cut those strings that bind you to a life of pride and earthly desires. Although it feels secure because you have a sense of control, there is no freedom in that. Cut the string and walk in the free life I died to give you."*

What does being a puppet mean?

"When you react or do things in response to someone else instead of your calling or purpose- not to follow or be played like a puppet without importance."

John 1:12-36 *"I went away so that others could follow Me. Although your were not here when I walked the earth, I Am here with you now. Man limits himself to what he sees. Faith is the substance of things hoped for but yet unseen. Why walk blind? Open your eyes of faith. The light I guide with is bright and there is no need to fear stumbling when your strength comes from Me. Watch for those who come in My Name, but do not know Me. They are of the liar and need to know truth. My love and words I spoke in scripture shatter lies. Share this truth in love not in condemnation or as a battle. I have won. They need to see the Father in your eyes when you tell them of My love."*

John 1:37-43 *"Human praise feels good. It gives you a false sense of worth. Poison tastes sweet at first but it only knows one path-death and destruction. Do not fall for earthly praise-seek Me first in the morning before you go out and ask Me to guard your heart and strengthen your faith to do My Father's will despite man's reactions. They are mere ants on a hill compared to My Father's power."*

John 1:44-50 *"My Father's Words are life. Go out in My strength and be a witness to what you have heard and seen, many don't know Me or have only heard of Me. Because man sometimes prostitutes My Father's name for their glory- they reject Him and Me. You know Me and My Father and our true identity. When you walk bound by the enemy or by man- you are not revealing the Father in you. I Am freedom, peace, joy and hope for your future. Go out in confidence-I Am with you. Be still and know my Lordship has not changed. Although some will challenge your faith and My existence."*

Ezekiel 11:1-12 *"I need you to stand firm for the righteous. Do not give up and give in because people don't have the same standards.*
Their baring is based upon what they know, not who they know. They don' know Me therefore they have no moral compass."

Why does it seem like the people who do what they want get away with everything and those of us who are trying to do what is right feel run over? How can we be humble and yet respected?

"Their pride blinds them to truth. Even if you do/say everything correctly, they have a skewed viewpoint. They cannot see what you see. It's not them that you need respect from, it's Me. When you do what's right and you love in the face of adversity it honors Me."

"How can you trust that My Word is Truth? How do you know when you can't see Me?

> *I AM: -all around you.*
> *-watching and encouraging you.*
> *-seeing you fall and holding your hand.*
> *-waiting for you to give more of you to Me through faith.*
> *-your loving Father who won't ever leave or disappoint you.*

Although you can't see the wind you can see its effects and feel it. When you feel the wind, let it remind you that I haven't gone anywhere, I AM with you. You are My daughter worth more than you realize. Keep Me near; know Me for who I AM not what you have heard I AM. Draw to Me, don't fear Me. I will give you rest."

1 Peter 2:11 *"Your flesh is weak and will fool you into thinking fading things are valuable. Just because something seems good, doesn't make it so. If it is followed by guilt afterwards it's not of Me. These are snares and traps that keep you distracted.*

Peace comes from within. It's knowing that there IS NOTHING to fear, because I truly am with you. I walk beside you and cheer for you to be brave.

Read my Word and believe it in your heart so you know Me for who I AM and that I stand for righteousness and love of all people. Not one was created superior to the other. All are equal in My sight. Competitiveness comes from insecurity and is useless. Competition that trumps loving someone is pride.

Your gifts you have been given are enough. You feel as though you are never enough. Develop your gifts instead of discarding them as worthless. When you focus on your gifts and strengths you will flourish. Looking to others for affirmation is a trap. They have their own issues and are consumed by them and have no affirmation to give you. Instead draw near to Me, develop your strength and comfort from Me so that you can be full and overflow with blessing for others who are weak.

I will not "perform", but I will talk to you. Don't waste effort wondering- I AM HERE."

1John 1:1-2:11 *"You wouldn't think that darkness can blind you. Darkness not only prevents you from seeing Me, it causes you to stumble and fear the unknown. You fear because I AM not in those places and I have put that fear in you to keep you away from those places that are not of Me. When you get the urge to flee a place, ask Me to confirm it I will never lead you on a path of destruction but to a place of abundance and joy. Life is not just breath in your nostrils. Obtaining all life has to offer, living is FREEDOM. Freedom from the cardboard reality that the enemy wants you to believe. There is no power in the enemy's portrayal of the truth. Don't be intimidated, look at it from the side and it will reveal it as merely a prop with weak footing that can be blown over. Stand firm in Me-look at Me from all angles-you will see I AM the same everywhere. I have and always will be: I AM."*

1John 2:15-17 *"Accomplishments are great, but they shouldn't be your goal of life. Make Me your goal- to trust and know Me more. To let your guard down and walk in My dwelling place."*

1John2: 18-27 *"You continually get surprised that I show up and speak. In a devotional written by someone close to Me or in My Word written in the past. Let your seed of faith flourish and grow-don't walk away from it. I know it's scary and can't seem real. That's because it's not of this world. It seems foreign- but it is authentic. Seeking Me daily for strength and renewal is not weakness, its wisdom. When you abide in Me is when you are at peace. That peace draws others to Me because there is no peace in this world. The enemy causes people to strive, I want people to thrive- full of peace/joy/love."*

1John2: 28-3:24 *"I'm dwelling in you when you believe in Me. That's where the struggle comes in- the flesh vs. Me."*

1John4: 1-5 *"People of the world are ruled by the world because the ruler of this world rules them. He is not of Me and is a liar. Therefore, don't let the standards of this world ruled by a liar define and control you. Lies are death. My Way is life. Don't be deceived by this world- it's ruled by a liar and many who come against you are coming against you because they have fallen for the lie and are controlled by the father of lies. If you are "failing" according to this world- chances are you are in Me. I'm nothing like this world. I AM all things pure/hope and expectation of things to come. That is why you are light in the darkness. Light draws attention to itself because its meant to stand out and draw people to the source of this light which is Me. Don't dim your light, thinking you are not like them and need to conform, NO. You are called to stand out for Me and draw them to Me."*

1John4: 6-8 *"My love has nothing to fear because it is perfect. Abide in Me-shine bright for all the WORLD to see."*

"Everything that is not perfect is not chaos. When you get distracted by the things that don't matter, you miss out on the things that matter most. The reason chaos scares you is because you think you are in control when all things are going your way. Look outside what you can see with your eyes to what can only be seen by the spiritual realm. There's a battle being waged for your attention and you fall for it every time."

"Take yourself off the field and see the game from a spectator. You put yourself on the field with imaginary goals to obtain and the enemy keeps tripping you up. These are not even the real goal of life."

Then, how am I supposed to live and view my life?

"The path is not important and the goals are not what makes life a win. It's being present in the moment and being at peace because you are <u>with</u> Me. Where we go is not what's important, its who finds us along the way."

I don't know how to live without a goal and just wake up with no plans or things to achieve and accomplish.

"Those things are not bad, it's when you let the enemy bring you down for not achieving them. Remember, the <u>goals</u> are <u>not</u> what's important, it's the people <u>along</u> the path The people who are hurting or are loosing at their "life goals." When you come along side of them you share My peace that's inside of you. That's why you have to be available to walk a path that's not your own, when you realize life is not confined to goals, but people your path can take you to limitless locations and help many people along the way. Don't fear rejection, it's not normal for people to REALLY care. Be consistent and patient with those you come across on your journey. Remember it's not a race to get to the finish first. That's a deception of the enemy. It's a slow stroll down a beach or mountain trail. Be at peace <u>in</u> your walk. People on the trail/path need encouragement and hope. I know the desires of your heart, when you help others know Me you are helping to grow the Kingdom."

I love you and am thankful you want to be seen/known/heard. Thank you for the smallest of details that remind us that everything will be ok and that you are in charge.

Is this generation different from those during biblical times?
"No. Inventions get made, wealth is acquired but the same theme remains. Self absorbed. Some self-indulgence is acceptable, you need to love yourself. But when you only focus on yourself you begin to be unsatisfied with what you have, who you are and what you thought you would have achieved by now. Define your life "Big Picture" and live within those parameters.

Draw a spiral that radiates out from the word Self.

Now on the 4 corners of the spiral write:
Caring about others
Faith that allows you to stretch
Confidence in who I made you to be
Pray for others more than yourself

This is not a binding trap; this expands out like the galaxies- limitless opportunity because you are not hindered by self-absorption. How often do you think about yourself? Have you given Me your requests and fears or are you wanting to just look at them and live in fear?"

"People don't know Me because they don't seek Me. I AM here. I AM willing. Sometimes it's the small things that you admire that I reveal myself in: tiny hummingbird feet, beautiful sunsets and faint breeze. Other times it's through an affirming word from a friend who was lead to tell you. I AM big and I AM strong, but I choose to be gentle. People who are intimidated need to show their strength. Those who are confident in their strength have no desire to flex it. No one walks up to an infant and flips over a table expecting the baby to be impressed.

Strength comes from within. It comes from knowing who you are and what you stand for. It's not a physical thing, its mental. You can develop physical strength but it shouldn't be to mask an inner weakness. When I call you out upon the water, to get out of the boat it's not on your strength to stand. It's Mine. The water represents things of this world that trap us and ensnare us. It's been _defeated_ and lifeless. Quit bringing it back to life by giving it power. The water becomes friend and a play place when you are lead by Me. Nothing to fear because you have Me. People are afraid to trust is why the "get out of the boat"-"Oceans deep" illustration is so impactful. There's actually nothing to fear. The issue is trust. Do you TRUST Me as your LOVING FATHER who knows all to come? Do you trust My plan for your life? Ask for the faith that you lack. I see it- it's not a surprise to Me. I'm not mad, I want you to live free and walk bravely holding My hand. Things you desire that are good will come your way. Things of this world seem like they are harmless and fun, but they damage your character and defile you like trampling on a beautiful white wedding gown. You are made for so much more than trivial silliness. Get out of that filth and give Me your gown. I will make it new. You are worth it. You are the daughter of the King - I _have_ called you mine.

Be excited. We have fun places to go in your new dress."

Matt. 21:14 *"When people admit their weakness no matter how obvious and come to Me it can be healed. You have to first realize that you are as strong as you allow Me to be in your life."*

John 18:14 *"Through My death and sacrifice came many blessings. Sometimes people try to hurt you for their gain, but the Father uses it for His glory."*

1 Peter 2:11 *"When you belong to the Father you are foreigners of this world. This world tries to conform you and lead you astray through fake senses of worth and value."*

"Read John's letter about Me and My life. Tell Me what you learn about completely living for the Father."

Dear Lord- open our eyes and ears to hear from you Lord. Teach us your ways and help us to understand your Word. In Jesus name. Amen.

1Peter 2:11 What does it mean to abstain?

"Don't give them a foothold. Don't think you are controlled <u>by</u> them. When frustration, anger, lust, rebellion, fear and denial rise up in you- claim victory over it in My Name and move on. Right now they overcome you and it shouldn't be in your life with Me."

You feel weak and let others dominate you. It's a copout. You have My inner strength. Don't cower down below the table I've called you to. Take my hand and eat at the table with Us. Many of Us are here, enjoying the feast The Father provides. You have to be willing to take your seat that has already been set for you. Until now you've lived a life groveling for crumbs beneath the table. Take My hand and your seat. Many are here at this feast. Look around- many fathers of faith, some who were with Me not written about in My Word, some are new to the faith and are already sitting here. It's peaceful and abundant in this place. No one lacks a thing. You deserve this place and abundance- claim truth over the father of lies and rest."

"Rest in My wings and lets fly. There are many places I want to take you but your heart is heavy dwelling in the past and how others treat you. Remember the path I showed you- the people are along side you, don't look to the right or left, be at peace and walk with Me. Gifts and talents you once used will spring up with new life and fuel others. When you look at the place you used to be- know that you are where you are supposed to be now. That trials in the past and growing in strength and faith brought you here now-for this time. Think growth and resurrecting strength and hope. My joy is in you."

"Like the distracting call of the crow at the top of the trees during your quiet time, mistakes in the past fight for your attention. They call them mistakes but they are not. They are part of the stage and foundation that you now stand on. Stop giving power to those who don't deserve it. No one should be over you and your walk with Me. When the crow of "failure" tries to distract you from Me- just walk the other direction knowing he has no power but to distract. Don't give it to him and he will fly away."

"Pop the pity party balloon and walk with Me. The perceived weakness and lack of recognition comes from your choice to sit on the floor in contempt of those at the table. They are not better than you. It's pride that has you down. You grovel and pride yourself on how hard it is working but your working is groveling. Stand up, pop the balloon and sit at the table of abundance. They are not above you and should have no authority over you. They are willing to take what has already been given. You live in a prison that you created from fear projecting out restricted strength as though someone else is holding you back but really its you. You like and feel as though you are not worthy to be at the table because you don't have what others "seem" to have: intellect, beauty, confidence, joy and peace. Just be willing to cast these chains of meekness and walk in My strength. Your wings are full of My spirit. Lets fly in them and see who you really are. Not what the liar has said you are because of what you fear you lack, but the daughter I made. She's beautiful and complete because you are Mine."

"Now that you are seated at the banquet table with Us, look around. What do you see?"

Abundance. Comfort in those around me. Stillness- no sense of needing to BE anywhere else.

"This is your "center." When the world tosses you back and forth, come back to the table and find rest. This place is like no other. It's full of all your desires and dreams. It seems like it's just a place to share a meal with other believers, but its My Father's banquet of blessings. Don't give away your seat here because the enemy causes you to believe a lie. No one else can have YOUR seat, because it is yours alone. Know your position in The Kingdom. The enemy is beneath My feet, trampled by My death and resurrection. The enemy's punishment in the Garden of Eden was to crawl around in the dirt. Your groveling days are over the minute you accept Me as Lord and Savior. We have a seat reserved for you at the table. The enemy isn't threatening or scary and his lies seem dumb from a view at the table."

SUN STAND STILL LORD
Reveal to this generation what you've got. In Jesus name-Amen.

Joshua 11:12
"Doing My will is never easy. Sometimes there are "Royal" strongholds that must be put to the sword for you to move forward in your faith. Be strong and trust in My Strength."

1Peter2: 11 *"Wage war against your soul."*
"You are showing up to battle unprepared. Your getting knocked down because you didn't realize there was a war going on for your soul. Great things can be accomplished in your life by My strength.
Distracting crows call for your attention away from My calling on your life. You hear and see their friends agreeing with their disruption of your calling. They are merely <u>distractions</u> in your life. They are not greater than I, they can only distract if you allow them to."

"With a great calling, comes great faith. You must not walk in this world looking without spiritual vision. There's the world you see with your eyes and there's the world you see though faith. Faith takes trust. Just because you are not _seeing_ results right now with your eyes doesn't mean I'm not working. Be bold and trust. Believe in Me for what I've planted in your heart."

How do I walk looking through "Spiritual" eyes and not get frustrated by the "crows" of this world?

"Know they are weak and insignificant, they are merely created beings. I Am eternal. I Am all-powerful. If you don't know how to tap into My strength you will remain intimidated by dust. See them as I see them-DUST. Nothing is intimidating about dust. Jesus told His disciples to shake the dust off their shoes and move on to a new town. Dust off the people who mock and persecute you, who annoy, frustrate and even distract you from _Hearing_ Me and BELIVEING in Me and your _specific_ purpose for your life. In Me there is life in abundance. Faith moves mountains and shakes off dust."

"I AM not a mystery to those who seek Me. They see Me, but are afraid because they see My power and submission I require. Love them; trust in Me that I Am working. Listen more than you speak- build a foundation for them to come back to. Don't be anxious-that's not Me. Loving in the moment, praying for words from Me and having the faith to cast that seed to the person that's seeking is doing My will. The enemy tries to come in and snatch the seed through doubt and condemnation as though you were not enough. Just rest in this place after you cast the seed. Hear the supernatural sound of people praying for the lost to be found. That's the internal rhythm and breath of life. Breathe in and out in peace of this rhythm. Join those who are already praying to find Me. Pray they let their guard down and are willing to explore more about Me as Creator. Not merely that I exist, but that I have called them by name for a purpose in this life only they can fulfill. Don't get discouraged by their understanding of My occurrences as coincidence or weirdness. They are comparing it to what they know and can relate to. Be happy for them- I Am near, I Am working."

Ephesians 4:11-16 *"You all have been given different talents and strengths. Each strengthens each other. Never be jealous of someone else's strength. If your calling required it I would have given it to you. Mighty warrior of God, stand strong in your faith. My wings are in you to soar."*

What does that look like? How do I live like that? Compare it to have I've lived so far...

"You are a mighty Oak full of strength and power- your roots go deep beneath the surface. See yourself of your faith and strength you get from Me. When you go out hold your head high in confidence because I AM with you. When circumstances or people cause you to tremble from fear, intimidation or frustration- call on Me and go back to your inner peace. Walking with Me. Crows distract and are made of dust. Remember to seek Me in your day, not just in the morning but also in all conversations and circumstances. Things will be difficult in this life, but I AM here to help you see the hope that is in Me and who's power you possess."

"You are here for a reason. You are not insignificant. I called you to a purpose ONLY you can fulfill. Be calm in My strength. Don't waiver when times are tough. Keep your focus on Me."

Ps 21:11

"My strength is not in them, but they often win the war because My strength is not utilized. Your strength in Me is often forgotten when they come at you. Remember they are mere cardboard cutouts and have no depth. Look at your enemy from all angles to see there is no substance to them. Once you see that they are truly weak, they are no longer a threat or distraction, not even worth wasting your thoughts or time on trying to make them like you. Move on, pray for them. Pray they seek Me and My strength, not the strength they feel they've earned and should be recognized for. Anything born from pride is not of Me. I seek My Father's will and so do all those who walk with Me. There's room at the table for those who wish to seek His face."

"Why read what My Father wants for your life? Why take the time to read what was written so long ago? Because it is timeless. It is alive and the pages know no bounds. Seek Me with your heart and ask Me to speak and explain the scripture and it will be done. This woman sharing her faith and experience with you now was just a willing vessel. Because she was so transformed by her experiences she wants you to have the same. Her heart was completely open and let Me in not knowing what I would say, but she KNEW I would speak. That's all it takes is a willing heart and I will do the rest. Pray that I become the priority in your life and that I AM the place you draw strength and comfort from. That peace is what you feel when you read My Word, that pages would come alive and your faith would burn like a raging fire that can only be fueled by time with Me in the Word. I AM there and I Am in there. I AM eternal but yet I seek your face, your friendship, your trust and love."

"There are some of you who feel unworthy because of your faith, because of your past and some because of what you did last night. I AM the Father of love. I know your heart and I also know your deeds. My heart seeks you despite your deeds. When you give me your sins, and ask to remove them they are <u>no</u> MORE. I have forgiven and forgotten them. You want to walk around holding onto them in a sack that you can pull from as an excuse to not feel qualified to show your faith in Me. Those filthy rags no longer belong to you. Stop going back to them. I have called you daughter and My daughter is clothed in righteousness that comes from Me. Cast that bag you carry around that's full of guilt, shame, un-forgiveness, doubt, self-loathing, hypocrisy and anger into the sea. Let's walk together in peace, love and joy. Your time here is not about condemnation for past mistakes, missed opportunities or even fear of failure and rejection. Your time here is meant to be in close fellowship with Me so you can walk by faith and not by sight, so that others can feel Me in you-Daughter –cast it now.

Cast all those burdens over the cliff into the sea and let's go. Where do you want to go? Where do you want Me to take you? What are you needing that only I can supply? Dare to ask it. Claim it in My name that I will provide. Remember that things are at work even if you are not "seeing." Trusting Me is being willing to accept no for an answer if it's not My Father's will.

Don't let the outside influences well up and overcome you. When you see something or someone overwhelming you or starting consume you- picture yourself as a glass filling with liquid. Keep the liquid below and pushed down into perspective. Right now these influences come and take over your being. Remember they are not Me and don't have the right to take over your house and My temple. I AM stronger. Don't let them cause you to forget. When you feel out of control because of circumstances or problems, picture Me draining the water away and relieving your fear of drowning. You have to claim your victory in Me everyday and let Me rule over your circumstances. All the authors in the Bible had their circumstances and issues they dealt with on a daily basis too, but they chose My strength in them over the fear and rejection and hurt that was surrounding them. The Words written were written in the past, but they were written by obedient servants of My Father for you and all generations to come. Some of the pages are history, some of the pages are poetry, some are the pages have yet to be fulfilled, but all of the pages are life. Life is not about things/achievements/goals/desires. Life is dwelling in My Father's harvest and letting Me consume all of you. Not withholding things because you are ashamed- I see those too. Hand them to Me and lets move on. Stop wanting to secretly fail. You think that by having something as an excuse to hold onto for failing is safe, but really its just lack of faith in Me. I never fail. Things and people may fail, but I never fail and I will never fail you. Just because you are not getting the result you want right now or at all doesn't mean I'm not working on your behalf. TRUST is not asking Me to work out all the issues related to your plan. Trust is saying Ok-I'm willing."

Lord, show me what you want me to do in this life you created me for. Open the doors you want me to walk through, don't let me fear the crows who cry out to distract or startle me from seeking you.

"A new way of living is budding and about to bloom in your life. You are going to cast away the things that used to take priority over Me and seek Me because we are best friends and you wouldn't dream of going out alone without Me. New things are taking place. Even in the faith you have shown to seek Me thus far. Ask Me for guidance, give Me your trust, dreams, even little insignificant things and see what takes place. I make all things new for those who do not seek the glory for themselves. Humility is knowing that you were <u>created</u> for a purpose by the Father. A loving and patient Father who wants you to live a life filled with abundance and a harvest of believers who know Me because of your willingness not to keep it silent. In your hallways, in your workplace, in your families- sit up tall and claim your inheritance I gave you- don't grovel at My Father's table on the floor. You were called to the feast that He provides. The enemy says you are lucky to <u>get</u> the scraps that happen to fall from the table, that others who are more qualified are only "worthy" to sit with Me here. But I'm calling you to this table where your seat has always been reserved for you and you alone. It's ok to let Me love and honor you at this feast. You <u>are</u> worthy because I invited you. Confidence in knowing you ARE ACCEPTED and wanted is not arrogance or pride. It's merely <u>living</u> out life in abundance and being willing to accept the inheritance I left you. <u>Guilt</u> free. I'm <u>not</u> mad at you. I'm <u>not</u> disappointed in you. You are My daughter and I want for you to sit at My Father's table with Me. Get up. You are <u>loved</u>."

Ephesians 5:1-20 *"You are My daughter, whom I clothed in white. When your actions are not of Me they stain your gown. Give Me your sins, your immoral thoughts and deeds and I will restore the beauty from your ashes. Small sins that you think are small are the same as what you call big sins in My eyes. If it's not of Me, it is of the father of lies. He has deceived you into thinking they are small. I cannot bless things that are not of Me. I cannot bless you and remove those stains if you are comfortable wearing a stained gown. You deserve a pure white gown I can give you from repenting. Every sin is equal in My sight, don't live like those who are far from Me and say "I just need to talk to someone about this." That is gossip, backbiting, betrayal and slander. Talk to Me first, ask for My guidance then take it to the person to give them a chance to fix the issue. If they shrug it off and it needs to be made right, take it to the person who oversees them. If the person who oversees them dismisses it too and it has not been made right I will handle it from there. You have done your portion, which is to honor your enemy by not sinning against them. You have done what I asked of you and I will control the outcome. It's difficult when people hurt you and seem to be able to get away with things you can't get away with, but I have given you a higher calling. I have called you to lead by example. If you look in amazement on others who are "getting away with things" you are falling for the enemy's trap of distraction. You are not them, you are not accountable for their actions they are. Forgive them and give it to Me to be healed in your heart."*

It doesn't seem fair; I can't help but to be resentful and even bitter.

"Bitterness and anger are not of Me. Which is better? To prove that dust was wrong or fellowship with Me? Anger, bitterness and resentment are stains for your gown. Hand them to Me in exchange for peace knowing that I see their deeds and their frustration they cause for you. I see your hurt. I will fight for the righteous, but I can't fight for those who have rebellion in their heart because <u>they</u> want to be the one that rights the wrong. Give Me your bitterness, anger and resentment."

John 21:1

"Do you see Me? Can you hear Me when I call you? Don't fear Me. I AM good. I AM there with you, although you may not realize it. At some point you are going to have to trust that it is Me and that I Am good. I will wait."

"Your wedding day is near. You are my bride whom I love. Lets sing and rejoice in the celebration at hand. This wedding is an everlasting covenant between you and Me- I won't forsake or leave you. I will honor your desires as long as you honor My Father and His desires. Are you ready? Are you ready to go after Me with your whole heart? Take My hand and let's go. Lets see what is out there for you to explore. I Am good and many blessings will flow from My Father through Me to you if you allow Him and I into your secret place. The place you guard. The place no one has been allowed to go. The deepest fears-things you fear others will find out about you. The place you store up that box of regret and shame. Lets remove that burden that surrounds your heart and makes you feel unworthy. I see all these things and I love you the same. They are not a surprise-I watch you guarding them and keeping them stored away. It's time. Its time to be free of that weight. Take them out one by one. Call them out and ask for forgiveness for each one and watch Me demolish that sin and crumble it to dust of the earth."

"Now, with the breath I put into your life, hold the dust in your hand and blow it into the wind and watch it vanish. There's no guilt. There's no shame-only My power alive in you, freeing you from those chains and weight that kept you tied down and intimidated for fear of someone knowing what was hidden in your heart. Let them all go. Even the ones that have deceived you into thinking they are your comfort zone. Things that are not of Me need to be removed from this place. You are more valuable to Me than you realize. Let's start over. Now that they are all gone-you might feel afraid because those things took your attention and gave you a sense of purpose-even if that purpose was to hide those things so that no one would know the real you. You have been made new. Your inner vessel has been removed of all those lies and burdens. Look at your beautiful heart. It's like a handmade sea glass vase. Realize its value and beauty and guard it. Only things that are of Me are allowed in this place. It's delicate and special. Find Me. Let Me fill your cup with who I say you are."

"Lets start by looking in the mirror. Find a mirror, and introduce yourself to My daughter. You are not the person you used to hate. You are not the person you used to be. All those things in the past are gone. You gave them to Me and asked for forgiveness and now they have vanished. Look in the mirror at your beauty. I see such beauty when I look at you. Your beauty is not determined by your outward appearance but by My love that is now able to radiate from within. Now look at your physical appearance. Love her. She is beauty- you are My bride clothed in white at her wedding day. Radiating happiness and joy, strength and beauty. This is the confidence you should pull from everyday. Not what the world says but who I call you: Mine."

"Be filled with joy. My joy is for the taking. Daughter we have so many things to discuss. Are you ready? We need to be as one. When I move you need to follow. You won't know I've moved if you don't hear Me calling you to a new place. Draw near to Me and listen. Listen first before you move. Seek Me and I will respond. There's life in My Word. If you find yourself frustrated its because you haven't sought My counsel. Where are you? Where do you want to be? Are you bold enough to ask Me to make it happen? Why don't you think you are worthy of your calling?"

Maybe it seems like I'm making it up and its just something I <u>want</u> to do and not <u>called</u> to do it.

"I put those desires <u>in</u> your heart. The real issue is that you don't feel qualified. <u>I</u> <u>AM</u> your qualifier- It's My power in you that says you are worthy. Don't fear. I have told you that I AM with you. I won't leave. Dare to ask for what your inner heart desires. Dare to ask Me to take you there, to equip you and prepare you for your calling."

Lord, you are so good. Your love for me astounds me. How the creator of the universe would be called friend. Someone who shows up and loves without bounds.

"Don't get distracted by others who have different talents than you. Just because you don't have their talent doesn't make you any less valuable in My sight. Cut the weight that keeps you living a burdened life. There are things holding you down and oppressing you. There are other things that you need to do in your daily life- chores, job etc. but don't think that they are a burden. Those are just the "worries of life" I talk about. It's only a "worry" if you give them that authority in your life. Do them with a fresh set of eyes and with a new purpose. Do them in anticipation of what I can do in the daily tasks of life. Don't let the task burden you and weigh you down- do them but look up and look around. Who needs to hear from Me? Who needs a different outlook on life or even someone just to be present in the moment and listen. No one truly listens anymore. You can't be available for others if you are consumed by dread because you are hating a task or responsibility. Instead approach those same small tasks in anticipation of what I can do with the mundane."

*"**I AM love.** Whatever does not love does not know Me. Love is not full of judgment, jealousy, envy or strife. Love is peace and joy surrounded in confidence that My Father is in control. Love doesn't fear another, love is without envy. Envy causes division. Division causes others to not know My Father's love. You want to love but also try to hold onto your ways. Your ways are not My Father's ways. You have to set aside things of this world and seek His face. His face is love and joy without limits. Can you love without limits? Has someone hurt you that you can't forgive- you have a limit on the love you are willing to show them. Love has no limits. Look at My Father's love...did He condemn you or did He redeem you? You cannot control others and how they treat your or how they respond to your love. The point is to love. Loving people when the world says to hold a grudge, to cut them out of your life, to guard your back, to secretly hate them because they rejected you is enduring the persecution. Persecution is not just in foreign places on a mission trip. Your mission is where you are now. I've called you to this place and these people. Don't think that you are failing because you don't see a favorable response. You don't love because of the response or friends you will gain. You love because My Father is love. Those who don't accept My Father's love need it most. Don't fear the rejection. Rejoice in it because their flesh is seeing it and is resisting it= you are making a difference. Smile in the rejection knowing your love is showing and is impacting them. Love without limits and let My Father guard your back; build your friendships with people who will build you up. Love does not mean to put yourself in harms way, it means forgive those who have hurt or rejected you-that's true love. When it makes no sense to forgive or to love, you do it because My Father loved you while you rejected His love. Before you knew Me, I was not in you but saw you. My love is above all things. The Father is in you now and His love radiates. Don't fall for the weak flesh that cries out wanting revenge, hold grudges or resentment. Give that hurt to Me and let go. I need you to love. Loving the ones the world calls enemy is LOVE."*

"Have you stopped long enough in your day to hear My heart on the issue? When you don't consult Me in your decisions they could be leading you astray. People of this generation only know of Me. Many of their fathers were not close to Me. Seek out to find Me for yourself. Don't rely on someone else telling you My ways. My ways are timeless, they are unchanging. The heart of My Father is in Me; I seek to do My Father's will. If you do not know the Father you do not know Me. Many will come baring false witness in My name. Who do they say I AM? A prophet? A wise teacher? I AM that I AM. There is no weakness to My strength. All you seek is within My power. Are you willing to let Me lead you into truth, even if your requests are denied and the answer is no?

True love doesn't seek approval or value from gaining something. Love is _being_ in the place you are. Knowing if you have been given My Spirit and He lives in you is enough. My Father's house dwells in you. Quit thinking you are poor, you need more and more of whatever "it" is. All the riches of this earth are mere ant piles compared to the glory and riches of My Father's love. You have a vault of His riches locked away in an attic as though it was something embarrassing because it was relevant in your grandmother's day. Why are you ashamed of My love as though it's not what you need? All of eternity has been sitting under blankets in the attic as though it was an embarrassing burden to have to store. You say-"Yes I have it" as though its old laundry you haven't had time to donate. When you don't understand its worth and power it is useless as laundry in the attic because you lack faith to dwell in that place and not be ashamed of it. Are you ashamed because you think it's antiquated and not relevant to your life's circumstances? You think the Scripture is just old stories of events and people from the past. Look again. But this time go up into the attic of your faith. Ask Me to reveal your inner heart of why you are ashamed of Me and think I'm merely a burden. The treasures and accomplishments of this life are _not_ lasting. My Word is life and power. No matter when it was written and who it was written by-I AM alive. Dare to find Me in the pages of the Bible. Dare to uncover the mysteries of My Word. Ask for Holy Spirit to teach you and reveal how the Word relates to you right now in your situation-for this day and this circumstance. Try it."

Holy Spirit- teach me your Word. Make it come alive in my life. I want to know you and I want my own relationship with you. I'm sorry that I felt you were irrelevant to my life. Teach me your Word, open my eyes to the treasures hidden inside. In Jesus name- Amen.

"Welcome back daughter whom I love. Do you see your value in My eyes? Do you know your worth in who you are? I don't value your accomplishments and goals you set, I value your heart and love for others and The Father. I know it is not your hearts desire to do this, but you need to know: when you continually focus on yourself and your flaws and insecurity it is a form of idolatry. Idolatry is anything or anyone who takes up your primary thought life. Why are you consumed with your flaws? You are beautiful and perfect in My sight. There is no one without fault except My Father. When you meet Me in heaven there will be no blemish or imperfection. Here, everyone has things they lack or would like to improve about themselves. Stop falling for the lie that _you_ are not enough. You are Mine and I called you-_just_ as you are. You are beautiful in My sight. You have qualities about you that other people need. Ask Me to reveal your purpose I have called you to and lets being to focus on others. Put down the mirror of rejection and look at My hand stretched out to hold you. You _are_ beautiful. Hear My voice about this not the father of lies voice who wants to burden your life by filling you with thoughts of failure and weakness.

You are strong.
You are beautiful.
You have a calling only you can fulfill.
You are My beloved."

Psalm 21:1

"Do you believe that I died for <u>You</u>? Do you believe I would have died if it had <u>only</u> been <u>you</u> to die for?"

"Don't hate your regrets, failures, weaknesses. Give them to Me and lets do something new. Remember, thinking on things continually is a form of idolatry. Don't be consumed by self-loathing and hate. Let Me have the things you hate about yourself.
List them out one by one and let Me have them. Include the deepest regrets and deepest fears about your life:"

"Thank you for your willingness to clean out the burdens that keep you from your calling. Rejoice in knowing that I Am a good Father with many blessings for your life waiting to be revealed. Walk out in the gown you were given as My bride-full of grace, beauty, strength and My love-which radiates from your face-because you know <u>who</u> you are, because I say you are <u>My</u> daughter."

"You ask- how could I be your bride and your daughter at the same time? The bride is the church. The church is those willing to go out and share My love to others who don't know Me. The church is a place of love and strength for those who are lost and lonely. They have no father because the father they have listened to is the father of lies. I have brought them to you for healing- you are My church/My bride/My daughter whom I love. Show the lost this love that I have revealed to you. One that is without limits or expectations, only hope you seek My will for your life and not seek approval from man. By man I mean, all people. People have flaws- My will for you is perfect. What do you seek? What do you want to know from Me? Dare to ask, dare to hear what I say, dare to follow Me where I take you. How do you know it's Me? Is it coming from love? Do you feel qualified to do it in My strength? Ask Me to open the door and walk through it if it is My will for you. Ask Me to shut the door if it is not My will for you. Are you willing to trust Me in either circumstance? What if the door is shut and that was what you wanted? What if the answer to the question you wanted to be yes, was no? Do you trust that because I love you the answer has to be no sometimes? Your calling has to be based upon two things: 1. Trusting that I Am leading you to a life of abundance and complete joy, happiness. 2. Willingness to go where I lead you.

*It may not be a foreign land at first. It might be within your own household. **Just because the first steps might be small doesn't mean your calling is not great.** Be obedient in each step and be willing to go when I call you. It might be to the next table where someone feels alone and needs a friend. That's My will. <u>Love</u> without concern for your gain or acknowledgement. Love because there are so many other daughters of mine who are far from Me and may not even know I care. Be bold in the little things. Small steps are huge in My sight, because of faith it took."*

"Hear My Words daughter- you were called to this place. You were called to bring light into the darkness. Learn My heart and who I Am from those who wrote about Me and for Me long ago:

2 Peter 2:1
"If you do not <u>know</u> Me, how will you know when someone is telling you a lie about Me? Who do you think I AM? What do you know about Me from your own experiences? Not from what others have said, but you have felt or come to know about Me on your own?
"This is who I AM:
    Abba= *Father* **Romans 8:15-16**

    Everlasting
    - *Love for you.* **Jeremiah 31:3**
    - *Priesthood and Kingdom* **Psalm 45:6**

    Elohim= *God*
    -One God who is 3 distinct persons: the Father, the Son, and the Holy Spirit. **Genesis 1:26**

    Savior: **Titus 3:4-7**

    Lord God: **Exodus 3:14**

    The Portion of Your Inheritance: **Psalm 16:5**

    Perfect Righteousness: **Deut.32: 4**

    Shield: **Psalm 18: 30**

    My Beloved Son:
    - The Word: **John 1:1-5**
    - Immanuel: **Isaiah 7:14, Matthew 1:23**

    First Born Over Creation: **Colossians 1:15-19**

    God In The Flesh: **Hebrews 1:2-3**

    Creator: **Hebrews 1:10-12**

Sustainer of All: **Hebrews 1:3**

Destroyer of Death: **Hebrews 2:14**

High Priest:
- *Who sympathizes with your weaknesses.* **Hebrews 4:15-16**

Intercessor: **Hebrews 7:25**

"Now that I have told you some specifics about Me and My character write what you've learned that you never knew about Me before this."

"Read **Hebrews** slowly at your own pace. Pray that your eyes and ears would be open to the Words and that you would retain My Words in your heart.

It's ok if there are things that are not yet understood. Keep going, they will be revealed when you need them."

"Many words I have spoken are sometimes hard to grasp. I wanted you to know My Son and His authority He has over this life. He sits at My right hand as judge, but His flesh is also the veil through which you walk through into My presence. He mediates for you and draws you to Me. Trust in Him, seek His face. Things of this life ensnare, but things of heaven are life everlasting. Let your burdens drop where they are and no longer choose to pick them up. Thinking about them and carrying them around is not solving anything, only weighing you down."

"Hope."

"Are you afraid to hope? Just because things have not gone your way in the past doesn't mean that I AM unfaithful. You stand in front of a mirror pointing out all of your battle scars and stomp your feet in fear of it happening again. Trusting in Me is not the same as blindly going out without My direction. Hope is knowing that I Am good and that My plans for you are good. If you have no hope, you don't trust Me. Things that have failed, things that have wounded you, circumstances you are in and have been in are all PAST.

Yes, learn from your mistakes, but also forgive yourself and give them to Me. Hope and **trust** that your life is not ruined or done, that it's just beginning. I make all things new. All things new. Hope and be glad. Ask and seek My face not My hand. When you dwell in My presence for Me and not what I can provide that's the greatest gift I can give you. In My presence all things are new. While you are here in this place and time, be in My presence and seek My face. Don't be afraid to go after Me wholehearted. Don't force things trying to accomplish. Be ok just sitting with Me in the calmness and the quiet. The enemy lies to you and tells you to hurry, work harder and condemns you saying you are not enough. Look at the person over there who tries ½ as much as you and yet they are "beating" you. This life is not a competition. This life is about peace, joy, hope and love. If you unplug the enemy and remove his ability to have a voice he just withers away. Once it's silent you will wonder why it's so quiet. Come to Me and rest in this place. Yes there are things I have called you to do and you are not late. There's time to spend with Me. My timing is perfect. If you give Me your heart and trust in My future for you, you will be filled again with hope.

Don't fear people. They are not Me. Ask for protection of your heart and discernment for their needs. You are not failing if they reject you. It's Me in you they see and don't understand. Remember to just be still and quiet. Wait for Me to guide you in words. He has been unplugged and left behind. Hope. Tell Me your inner secrets and dreams for this life daughter. I love you and Am here."

"When the enemy tries to get your attention think of headphones cast aside laying on the floor. You hear sounds coming out but its just "noise." It has no meaning in your life and has no power over how you feel. It is merely noise over in the corner. Feel My power and know he has been unplugged and cast aside. He no longer has any guidance in your life, has no ability to tear you down. He is mere noise. Walk away and smile knowing he no longer rules your thoughts and your actions. He is weak and can only cast out lies. If you choose to put the headphones back on and believe his lies you have renewed his strength over your life. He's a liar and has been defeated and merely tries to destroy those who know and love Me. Don't fear him, just realize his power is only strength if you give it to him. See the headphones and the yelling coming out to get your attention with words of condemnation and things of fear. They are lies without power. I AM joy, peace, love and truth. There's a whole new beginning for you now. My timing is perfect. You have nothing to fear. Rely on My strength and guidance and we will go out together."

1John4: 19 *"I loved you first. It's ok to love yourself. I Am proud of who you are. I know your sorrow from your mistakes. I knew them long before you made them. I chose you and now you hear Me."*

5:14 *"I've been here all along. I've seen and heard every request. Just because you are not getting an audible nose response doesn't mean I'm not there. I see you. I hear you. I love you."*

Haggai-

"My prophet to Israel long ago. His word spoke to the people in his day about a temple built with hands. I dwell in a new temple. The body of believers. Read Haggai, but consider your body as the temple. Are you ignoring it or worse yet are you defiling it with your life's choices and thoughts?"

"I AM with you, as I was there in the former temple. Your body is My temple you are My living stones. I know it's hard to believe that I Am with you and even dwelling within you, but I Am here. You invited Me in when you asked Me into your heart. Look around at the temple you keep Me in. Are you honoring My dwelling place with your thoughts and actions?

"My signet ring is a seal of authority and authenticity. The Holy Spirit is My signet ring/seal of promise on your life. It keeps you sealed with Me eternally. No one can take you from Me. I have sealed you with My signet ring of authority- Holy Spirit.

Do you see your worth in My eyes? I'm hoping that you are beginning to finally see what I have been telling you all along. I love you."

LOVE.

"How's that coming? Is it easy to do? Why? Are there things you feel other people deserve-outright lack of love toward them so they will know what they did to you? Love is a gift from Me. It is not earned and I freely gave it to you. My love was so strong I sent My son to cover your sins so you could spend eternity with Me. Love is not something you should ever use as a tool. Love just is. Love is not conditional upon how you were treated or if you want to. Love is who I AM. When you choose to love despite how you <u>feel</u> you are choosing to show them Me. Don't expect things in return or even use it as a tool to elevate yourself. Love is love for the sake of them knowing I Am good. There will be many whom you try to love and they reject you and even try to offend you in return. Remember it's not the response that's important. It's your wiliness to realize that giving and showing My love is the greatest reflection of Me. I will do the rest. I can see their hearts and yours."

"I'm still here- I haven't gone anywhere. I know you feel alone. Don't despair. Even though you can't see Me, I AM there. Your beauty amazes Me. You see flaws, imperfections, missed opportunities. I see perfection-just as you are. Grace, beauty and strength abounds in your wings. Come stand with Me at the edge of the hills-rely on My strength I've placed within. Float and soar in My strength- there's no need to fear the height or the direction- I'm guiding you always. Dare to soar, dare to dream and see where this strength will take you. I know you feel as though you are lost and have not found you're way yet. How do you know you are not already standing right in the middle of My will for you? You haven't let Me down, you are not off path. Dust that became beautiful flesh will fail sometimes, it doesn't mean you are a failure. I Am pleased with a daughter that seeks My face. I Am making all things new – rely on My strength for this life."

Why does it feel lonely and without a clear direction of <u>what</u> I'm supposed to be doing?

"Each of you have different gifts, circumstances and things placed on your path. When you seek Me and rest in My peace, you will <u>see</u> what I'm calling you to. You will just know- you won't even question it. Don't feel like you are just finding moments to be useful to Me. Seeking Me, walking in My strength and look for those who need Me is My will for your life- no matter <u>where</u> that takes you. Just because I know where each of you will go doesn't mean you need the specifics. If I wrote out each one of your life paths in these pages that wouldn't give you the opportunity to trust Me within your life-happiness, blessings, dreams and fulfilling My will for your life- it would just be a guide and seem like a rule book with no options. It's like deep water, swim around and enjoy the swim the ocean is My will for you- you can't go wrong because you were willing to get in and see what I had in store for you. Rest in the peace of just being in My strength."

"Some of you are on the shore and you are staring at the waves- too afraid to get in. You have tried a few times but then the waves over power you, you feel like you are making a mistake and turn back. Don't fear the limited. I Am all powerful- push further, go out where the water seems dark and threatening when your mind says this can't be right- I Am there too. It takes complete surrender to My strength to truly understand this world has no power over you unless you give it. These things circling you-threatening you each day- stealing your joy and causing you to doubt are just as powerless as the cardboard cutout version of your enemy. When you view them through My power and strength they are silly. My strength, wisdom and love for you is limitless. Do you trust Me? I'll wait till you are ready-there's no rush. I don't want you to feel burdened. My love for you is not about accomplishments, burdens or even proving your love for Me. Take as long as you need. I'm in no hurry. I have all the time you need. Take baby steps or big leaps- its up to you- its not going to impress Me either way- you have already won My heart and you cant be loved anymore. Talk to Me- get it out- fears, frustrations, worries even where you feel I have let you down."

How can you be so powerful and be so sweet? Why do you bother to talk to us and share things with us?

"I love you. I adore you and want us to be as one. The vessel I fill is overflowing with power that can also be gentle and calming to those who see Me in you. Stop letting things of this world call you to them first. You wouldn't go on a trip without planning for all the things you would need- treat Me the same way- seek Me first each day. When you are full you will overflow with peace, love, joy, patience and will not feel powerless to these things that have ruled your life and thoughts for so long. It's time. Be still. Stop running from Me. I only have great things for you- My love is authentic.

List out the lies that you have believed- the fears you have and those things that cause you to doubt I'm here."

Isaiah 41:10 *"When you seek Me, you will find Me. Be still and listen, I AM always there to hear you and reply. I will reply in different ways because I know what is best. You are quick to anger when My reply doesn't come as expected, but that doesn't deter Me from guiding you. I know it's because you cannot see what I see and know what I know. Why trust and rely on yourself when I Am willing to share with you My knowledge and understanding which leads to peace. Peace comes when you let Me reign over your life. I Am gentle and loving King who searches out those whom I can save and serve. I Am not a heavyhearted ruler writing to condemn, blame and burden. My Lordship comes from a place of love, not a place of dictatorship and fear. I have already won and defeated the enemy-Its already been won. So why do you worry and doubt? Why can't you walk, the land and rejoice in the victory I have won for you?"*

I confess to you Lord, I walk in my strength and think the outcome of my life is in my actions, choices and determination. As though I'm going to miss out, fail you or myself. I want to walk in humility with you-want to trust completely in you- not in my efforts but just simply walking the path with you enjoying the things along the way. Remove me from the fear people impose upon me as tasks, deadlines, problems, anger and judgment. Help me to walk out what you have taught me. Amen

"Close your eyes. Listen- I AM here in the silence. This road feels like peace- you are not worried where this road leads you or what might be hidden along the way-because you are with Me. Reach out your arms and feel with your fingertips the tops of the wheat that are ready to harvest. The harvest is not guilt; the harvest is unlimited life in Me-joy, peace and everything you need when you need it. It's already been given to you- now you just need to claim this land you inherited. Walk with Me your Father who gave you this land because you have been redeemed. There is unending laughter and peace in this place. There are things in My will for you along this path, but they are not difficult because I have given you My grace to endure and My strength to overcome. When this world tries to lie to you and jumps out from the tall grass as a predator- don't be intimidated or afraid- just keep walking- remember he has already been defeated and I have won. His sneers can only distract and torment if you listen or look. Let him cower back into the grass knowing he has no more influence over you because you have claimed your inheritance.

In the moment of trials, fear of failure, fear of man- stand here in this place and feel My presence and know the truth-The harvest has come and the enemy has been defeated you are no longer slave to man or fall prey to his threats- you are MY daughter and I Am with you and in you. Stand firm in your faith in Me. Nothing that comes against us shall prosper."

"I have given you big and beautiful wings. You haven't known they were there. They are dirty from dragging them because you didn't know what they were for. Lets dust them off and look at them in the mirror. They are huge and full of My power. They are also uniquely made for you. Each feather was placed for your specific purpose to make it along the road with Me. You need time to examine them and admire them. Look at the intricate detail of each one- know I placed them in perfection and adorned My daughter whom I love. Extend each wing and look out along the tip- the wings are not heavy- they are part of you; you just haven't known you had them. Now that you know they are there and were made just for you, now you need to test their strength. Hold them out over your fears and let My breath fill your wings to soar high away from the things that fight for your attention. When the wind begins to overpower you let go and give Me control- lean into the wind and trust in My strength. Nothing should scare you when you trust in Me- you are not going to fail Me when you seek Me and trust in My strength. Even if the outcome or answer that is returned to you seems wrong or as a failure- it won't return void because you sought Me in your day, not your strength. Now, you are sitting there with a set of wings on- you know you have them and you know no one else can have the set I made for you. Do you see your beauty? Don't compare yourself to others, wishing you had some feature they have. Your wings, crown and wedding gown are a gift to My bride. When you envy something another has or has been given its like looking at your gifts as though they are filthy rags. Its not something you have done intentionally, you just never asked to see how I created you and to see yourself in My eyes. Stand up-look at your gown and extend your wings and wear the crown I have placed on your head with a kiss. Never doubt My love for you, the strength I Am in you or your perfection I see when I look at you."

"Sometimes you feel like you are going through life, being pushed around. Like a child strapped in a stroller and someone is pushing you around. You are uncertain of where you are going and feel trapped because you can't get un-buckled. What if the person who was guiding the stroller was your father? What would change? Would you relax knowing that he wouldn't let anything harm you? Would you still want to do things your way just for the sake of them being your way? What if it were Me that guided your stroller and I had you buckled in because I know you were afraid and might try to leave, but leaving might cause you harm. Do you trust that the buckle is My love for you? It's not to keep you from doing things you want to do; it's to keep you from things you don't see yet that can harm you. You squirm and contort your back trying to get up, you even cry begging to get up. But if you are just still and wait and relax in the fact that I AM in charge and I AM guiding you in this life. When you feel trapped it might be for a reason- its worse where you want to go — because you don't see all the things I see, don't know all things I know.

Lets try something new together. I'm letting you up out of the stroller-you are an adult and are looking at Me standing behind the stroller. This stroller is not belittling- its showing your faith. If you choose to get back in, it's your trust in Me that put you there. Do you have the faith to buckle yourself in and trust Me where I'm leading you?

If you choose to sit back down and buckle your strap, know that it is Me looking out into your future, taking you to the places that are best for you-they may not be the places you wanted to go, but they are the places you needed to go. When you rest in this place of faith its peaceful. Not having to wonder where your food, drink, necessities of life will come from-this is child-like faith."

It's hard to "relax" because I feel like I'm not doing my part. *"You are doing things in your strength. You can't sit in the stroller and push it at the same time. Ultimately its trust and faith you need. Seek My strength and wisdom each day. Sit down and rest in My strength."*

"Draw near to Me when you feel alone. Draw near to Me when you have no one. Draw near to Me when you are reaching your goals, working for perfection, and trying to be brave. The things you attempt to do and be on your own without Me will always be less than if you had sought after Me- to come along side of you for guidance and strength.

It's ok, I understand, I AM a quiet still voice and the world is great at distracting."

Lord-

I give you my fears.
I give you my ambitions.
I give you my future.
I give you my doubt.
Replace these things with

Hope-you have a great future for me.
Peace-you are with me.
Joy- I am excited for the things you have in store
for me.

Stop me in my tracks Lord when I forget to seek your face. Forgive me that I have left you behind so many times before. I <u>know</u> you love me and that's all I need.

"Thank you for drawing near. Thank you for guarding your time with Me. When things get out of control, its because you haven't sought after Me first. I speak to people on a daily basis, but not everyone has ears to hear. They doubt My existence and doubt their calling on their life. The things you love, I planted those in your heart. Don't fear My plan for your life, I cultivate what I plant."

You are so gentle and sweet Lord, how is it that the creator of the universe with power of life and death in your words would take the time to be so gentle and close to those who seek you?

"I AM not intimidated by man and the things that snare you. My work is finished, the enemy has lost and I AM just spending time with those who seek Me. If you were at a football game and the score had already been shown- the winner had been announced and the victory had already been won- how would you sit in the stands? Would you have more confidence in how things would play out? Would you fear less and worry less because you knew in the end everything was working toward victory? Would you communicate to those people beside you differently? Care about them and truly listen to them and the needs they might share without asking for them directly?
People go through this life as though they don't know how it's going to play out. They constantly look to the left and right and look to people for signs, significance and re-assurance. But what they are missing is that it has already been written who HAS WON. Why would you attend a game sad and defeated if you knew the outcome was victory? You wouldn't. Why do you not trust what I say and that I AM for <u>you</u> and I have defeated the enemy- there's nothing he can do about the outcome of the game. He's merely a distracter for those who haven't heard the news of <u>who</u> is victorious. I won and because of your faith in My work, <u>You ARE</u> victorious too. Knowing you <u>are</u> victorious, now what? What would you do differently? Would you fear making bad decisions or would you seek Me first and trust the outcome? Life in abundance is available, but it comes from walking with Me, not seeking approval from man. Its not that I perform for you because I speak when you ask, it's because I'm waiting to get your undivided attention to tell you <u>it is going to be ok.</u>
No matter how other people view you I see the beautiful girl with a heart for the lost. Just because you don't have a degree in divinity doesn't mean you are less valuable in My sight. If I needed you to get that degree I

would have pointed you in that direction in the beginning. I didn't forget about you and you're not off path. The things you have gone through and fought through and your life experiences you need them for where I AM taking you. If I needed you to get a masters in divinity I would have sent you to that school, but I sent you out because you wanted to seek the lost in My name and you are seeking My will not accolades from man. Don't listen to the enemy distracting you and trying to tell you, you missed your calling and time is running out because that is a lie. You are obedient, you are seeking Me and you are right in the <u>middle</u> of My will for your life. When the enemy tries to make you feel inadequate or off track know <u>what</u> I <u>say.</u> You are <u>not</u> off track, you are not disappointing Me. Rest in this place walking with Me-knowing the outcome <u>is</u> victorious and the enemy has been defeated, all he can do is <u>try</u> to distract. But if you take off the headphones, cast them aside, you can also unplug his power source and render him powerless. He is defeated you know. Unplug him and tell him he's lost and no longer has the ability to influence how you feel about yourself or your life's calling."

In Jesus name, I claim victory over the enemy's lies of defeat and hopelessness. I claim my victory that Jesus died for me to have.

"Smile. I AM with you."

"Hear My Words of Israel. They stray from Me and seek idols and people of other beliefs. I spoke to them before I sent My Son and shared My heart and desires for their lives. Some listened, others did not. Be brave and of courage, just as Joshua and Caleb were. They knew what I had promised but the difference was they had the faith that I would fight for them in the place I had <u>already</u> given them. Many see the giant and fear they have not heard from Me. They loose hope or just leave without trying. If you have heard My voice in a whisper, in My Word, through song, through dreams, through visions or even through someone else. Hold on; don't flee from your inheritance.

When you are standing at the border of your inheritance and you see the bounty and blessing, don't fear the giants in the land. They too have been defeated they chose not to know Me or seek My will, so they must not intimidate My servant with whom I'm well pleased. When you see the charging giant, smile and take courage. It's not you who is fighting. I have a mighty warrior with wings twice your size with sword drawn, fighting for your honor."

Its hard to put myself in that spiritual place-mind of faith when its just everyday life and I'm faced with an obstacle that's blocking my dreams, passions and what I heard you calling me to do.

"No matter how normal the environment might be- work, home, school etc. My presence and your calling haven't changed. Just because you view church as holy and everywhere else barren-without Me, that doesn't change the truth. I AM Holy. Because of your faith in My Son, your body is My temple. I didn't call you to stay still and build monuments; I called you to go out. That's why you have hands and feet. So people can see My heart for them in <u>action</u>. When you face a giant, remember My servant whom I called to watch over you, remember My promise that the giant has already been defeated and you just need the faith to walk into your inheritance. Be strong and of courage- stop looking at all places outside of church as secular and without Me. That's what My believers are for, if you feel alone in this faith —witness My love for them and share My truth about who I Am."

Isaiah 55:1-3

"Many hunger and thirst without knowing what they thirst and hunger for. They seek and search day and night, spending their earnings on earthly things. Earthly things don't satisfy. They are actually stumbling blocks. When joy is found in the creation and not the creator it is fleeting. I AM an un-ending well. Deep and without bounds. This water is what satisfies your thirst. Your thirst is satisfied in My presence. The water is where I AM found. This place is not scary when you trust in Me-completely. Submerge yourself in My love —these waters. Feel My love surrounding you. I Am with you in this place of complete surrender. Many who feel alone don't realize My presence. My love knows no bounds; it is unending life in abundance. Take My hand and begin to feel the freedom that is abandonment to earthly things- achievements, accomplishments, possessions and status. Those are mere mirages-they seem like they are life to the fullest but when you get them you still feel empty. That's because My love is the only thing that truly satisfies. I know you hear it and even believe it but why don't you walk in it? Its because you are keeping Me at a distance- you think that the things of this life are your "job." Yes, work to earn wages, but don't fall for the lie that work qualifies you. I AM. The I AM has qualified you. You are worthy because of the job My Father called Me to do. Work for a wage, but work, study, play with eyes wide open. Be willing to ask to <u>see</u> Me and My work without fear. You have to be willing to want to see it. My work is all around you-ask for eyes to see. Ask to be equipped to do the job My Father called you to. This work is not about earning wages or worth- your worth has already been determined. You are not working for wages or titles, you are working in My strength- it will only require obedience and faith. Are you ready? Are you ready for life of abundance? Are you willing to let go of earthly things to see The Kingdom?"

Lord, open my eyes to see the things of The Kingdom on earth as it is in heaven.

"Kingdom Lovers,

My time has come —call those to Me in your realm of influence. They are eager to know Me more. They are in their shell, wondering if there is more out there. They see Me in others but think it's only for a certain few. My love is deep and sustainable for everyone. Most people stand on the shore and get distracted and afraid of the waves, but My waves will not overcome you, they will not destroy you. Total trust in Me- fighting against the natural- when your flesh says to flee because you will drown, that's where most give up. Push beyond the feeling of being out of control and abandoned. I AM near. Its scary to completely trust in Me beyond what your strength can sustain, but that's what faith is…TRUSTING in ME and relying on MY STRENGTH not yours. There are millions of you, but only one I AM. It's fun out here in the deep; your fear is silly when you walk in My strength. Just like a child in a kiddy pool- larger than the pool itself, hanging off the edges and face out of the pool, but still with water wings on. Would you be afraid? Of course not. You are setting on dry ground hanging over the sides of the small puddle of water. That's what its like for Me- your troubles do not frighten me and they are easy for Me- I AM much bigger than any fear you have. I AM much stronger than any struggle you will face. Do you trust Me to give Me your water wings and trade Me, for the wings I gave you? The water wings are man made because they fear being out of control. My wings come from worship. They have been there all along; you just have to use them. They are calming-like the seraphim in continuous worship, but they are also powerful- when you speak My name they fill your wings with strength to soar like an eagle. There is power in My Name. Rejoice, My Kingdom is near. You are walking in heaven on earth when you love My lost sons and daughters. Show them the deeper places- where complete trust in Me leads to a life without limits."

"You will go places that seem unfamiliar, but don't be afraid, I AM there. Beauty abounds in My love. I Am calling you to a place where all people are now-They won't seem to be like you at first but under the surface you are exactly alike. Be excited. A new day has come. Now. The now, the different, the bold day you prayed for has arrived. Can you hear them sing? The songs of the believers? Join them in the chorus with a light heart, cut the cords that have held you back. This day is unique because I have brought you here- you didn't know that I knew of this place before you were born, brought all of these people here at this time just for you. Stop feeling like you missed out- that you waited too long to *know Me- to truly let Me in. It's OK, time stands still with Me. I work through your faith and My strength no matter the timing or circumstance. Look around at the beauty. The harvest in the desert, where you once were a stranger, but I knew you would come to Me and that we would be close. I love you. Lets go find people who don't know My love."*

"Pride and arrogance withholds My blessings. If you think you can do things better than others, you are being arrogant. There are times that you might be better, but assuming and proceeding without seeking guidance leads to trouble. You need to submit to the authority that has been placed above you before you will begin to flourish. Stop thinking you are always right and listen to those who have more experience and knowledge. Stop trying to prove you are special to others. Approval from man is not important. If you are seeking Me first and seeking to be a blessing to those around you that's when you will flourish. The flesh causes you to think you can do it better than someone else. So? Even if you do it better than someone else and you lost the respect or relationship over it- is that worth it? Do you really think success is standing on someone else to get there? If you seek Me and in humility offer changes then others will want you to succeed and even give you a helping hand because they genuinely care about you. Moving forward change your approach. Ask opinions and listen instead of just jumping in and doing it your way. No one cares but you. When I correct your behaviors or habits its only because I love you. You asked for My love and My love doesn't settle for the sin in your life. Pride was the fall of man's first sin. Adam and Eve were given free will in My garden I made. Complete paradise without any want. They were given fellowship directly with Me, they chose to disobey. Pride filled Eve's heart. She wanted what she couldn't have, as though I had withheld a blessing from her. My love knows no bounds. If something is restricted or withheld its not good for you and will lead you down the path of destruction. Her pride put a wedge between Us and her. Her pride caused her husband to fall too and ultimately caused them to have to leave My dwelling place. I knew they would choose this, but allowed them to do so because you can't know My full extent of My love if you don't understand that I Am willing to send My Son/I Am willing to die for each one who is lost-but it must be them choosing Me. Not Me forcing them. Love is patient and My time is limitless- I can wait for you to come to Me when you are ready. Is pride keeping you from Me because you have listened to the lie about Me? What about what you have heard Me say? Don't be afraid to trust Me. I will never disappoint you —only love you as Father and friend."

Are you ready for close fellowship and <u>friendship</u> with Me? We love you-Father, Son and Holy Spirit- We love you and see beauty when we look at your heart and outward appearance. We are not here to pressure you into doing what We want but want to help you in all that you do. Ask for Our strength, power, wisdom, love- whatever you need is available. All you have to do is ask. We love all of you this way. Unfortunately pride takes on many forms and blinds people from seeing Us for who We truly are. Pride has even caused man to worship false gods, create idolatry and even worship themselves. When you think you are infallible, that too is idolatry. The correct posture is to understand you once were dust and We formed you so you could know Us and walk in fellowship with Us-knowing true love comes from The Father. Think of the things that amaze you- the stars, galaxies, maybe the ocean, mountains or even the redwoods in California. All the wonder and power displayed was created by My Son's Words. His Words are life and power. His Words filled your nostrils and breathed life into your lungs. You are My treasured possession. All the wonders on this earth that amaze you were only created to show you how much We love you. We had creation cry out so you would see Our power and you would hear Us calling your name. The universe is limitless and that displays how much Our love is unending, that beauty was created for you to realize Our power- limitless. It was formed from nothing. Just spoken Word. When Jesus came in the flesh He walked on earth as man and dwelt among you- when He left, He promised Holy Spirit to internally dwell in all Our believers. As believers He is inside of you, He has given you the mighty wings that propel you places you have gone and also comfort you when you are needing peace. Feel the slow beat and comfort of them slowly moving at rest. There's nothing too difficult for Us to handle. Give it over to Us- your trust, your dreams, your fears. We love you and are here for you."

"How long will you wait to truly know Me? Why do I scare you when all I Am is love? Although you have flaws and sins, My son died to cover those with My love.

I am here for you as Father, friend and Savior but you must trust in Me and give Me all of the things that keep Me from you. Un-confessed sin I cannot cover because it was not given to Me. When you confess your sins you are admitting what I already know. Just because I know it doesn't mean I AM not willing to draw close to you- I long to be close, but un-confessed sin keeps Me at a distance. If you want to be best friends, willing to sit face to face on the beach sharing hopes, dreams and accomplishments, blessings- everything together you have to let go of the things you already gave Me when you confessed them. I Am not looking at you with eyes of judgment and disappointment, I Am looking at you as a Father sees His daughter. Happy she longs to be near to Me and wanting to talk as long as she wants to.

Unlike earthly fathers I gave you, My time is limitless, My knowledge and strength is also limitless. All you need to bring to Me is faith in what My Son died for you to have- relationship with Us.

If there are things you need to tell Me do it as they happen so they don't build up and make you feel unworthy to be in My presence. Your life and works, sin that is intentional or unintentional never earned you this right. My Son gave that to you because He loves you too. So when you fear sitting face to face and are ashamed of what you think I might see, there's nothing to be ashamed of —I see your heart in your eyes, your sins and failures are not a disappointment. I knew you would make them. But here's where I will ask something of you- that you seek Me and My face first. That you would ask for My strength and wisdom daily and that you would confess your sins as they are committed so your life can be abundant, full of joy and deep _personal_ relationship with Me face to face without fear because your Father has called you to this place."

"Love who _you_ are. There are always people who seem to have more, have figured out life sooner and even seem to be "better" than you. The deception is that they are happy because of those things and who they appear to be. The truth is, they are not perfect. They have regrets, insecurities, failures, and even things they don't like about themselves too. Instead of being jealous of someone who has a trait you don't, be happy for them and compliment them for that trait. Tell them you admire them for that trait. True joy is loving others through Me- not attaining everything by effort. The view of yourself is not the way the world sees you. There might be times when you feel so small and insignificant, but you are actually strong, brave and something to behold. You are not helping yourself by regretting your weaknesses. No one is perfect and by hating things you are weak in only makes you feel like a failure or not enough. I AM enough. Wipe away everything- it's just Me and you together face to face- nothing else matters but the heart I see. Love yourself and let her live. If you did _nothing_ else, but love people for the rest of your life you will have lived a life I called you to live. There are many levels to people's calling in life. If you are brave enough to seek them and to go after them, and your heart and motives are pure; I reveal them as the time is right. Most people fear they missed out already, they are not qualified, they will fail when they get there, but what they are forgetting is that I AM. I AM enough. I AM the one that called you to this place and I never fail. You think that when things are hard, people are mean or when attempts fail, that you somehow feel off base or even have missed your calling. Actually you haven't. Those trials are designed to help you grow in those areas of weakness. When people are mean or difficult to get along with it's because you need to develop a deeper sense of self worth. You get to a place where people's attitude toward you doesn't change how you view yourself. When doors close, it's only Me guiding you to a more specific place. Remember, when you seek Me first, there's nothing that's impossible- seek to have your eyes opened to the truth of the situation or circumstance. Ask Me to give you strength, peace, patience and understanding. I love you."

"How long have you stood there in shame? Why do you feel as though I AM disappointed in the woman you have become? Why don't you believe that I love you as you are? My grace is enough for you, I have forgiven you long ago for the mistakes and sins you confessed but yet you carry them around weighing yourself down in shame and guilt.

My love is freedom. Freedom from shame and guilt. When you refuse to accept the beauty I clothe you in and want to walk around in sackcloth and ashes it disgraces My love for you. Why are you afraid to reveal who I see? You are nothing like your former self-before you knew Me. Today you are strong, brave and have such a strong heart for the lost and the least. Are you ready to lay down the guilt, shame, fear and inferiority complex? Close your eyes- We are here together- just Us. Now open your eyes and see the depth of your Father's love. Those rags you have clothed yourself in for so long no longer fit you-you have out grown them as though an adult is trying to wear toddler's clothes. They look silly on you and out of place because it's not you anymore. One by one, I AM going to take these from you and together We will eliminate them from your wardrobe. From now on you will only wear My clothes of righteousness that I gave you when you first confessed your faith in Me.

Lets first start with the cloak of guilt and shame.

Filthy rags have no place on My daughter. By wearing them it doesn't prove to Me you are sorry. I knew you were sorry and I forgave you long ago. Now you need to forgive yourself. I Am not disappointed in you. You <u>ARE</u> where I want you to be. I cannot lie. My Words are truth. If you believe in Me and My Words as truth you have to believe I have your life in My hands and I AM not disappointed in you. I love you and you are doing great. Give Me the rags you have worn of guilt and shame-they are no more."

"Next We need to remove the shield you hide behind- a mask of fear you wear because you don't see the strength I gave you. Everyone else sees it but you. You hide behind this mask of "fear" because you feel safe- "unqualified" to do more or be more. Unqualified to speak up and share your thoughts on things. It's a false idol. You wear this mask as your identity. It's your protection against being hurt, or so you think. You imagine yourself as weak and afraid- that others see you this way-all the time you are focusing in on the mask you put on for others to see.

Let me remove that mask for you. Close your eyes. You have a radiant face filled with My love for others to see. When you hide it under this mask it hides My love for them. Don't be afraid- just like a daughter is proud her dad has come to an event to share her day-that's how you should look because I Am always with you."

"There's one last piece of clothing that doesn't belong; your mouthpiece. You use it to say that you don't have a voice. My voice is in you and you hear from Me daily. Lets get rid of the mouthpiece that has become a pacifier- something that comforts you as an excuse. Pray before you speak- seek My wisdom and in faith just let the words come out. I Am throwing your pacifier into the ocean. You outgrew it years ago. Now-
I want you to take a look at yourself as I see you…
A woman of faith. Strong, confident, radiating My love in her eyes and smile. Trusting in My Words and My strength to guide her. There's no one you can't reach when you show the world this true image of Me through you."

"Your wings are beautiful like jewelry. They are colorful and unique to each person-but only I see the uniqueness. To the human eyes they are white but I see the colors I placed on each feather on each strand for your purpose because each one of you are unique in My eyes."

"My daughter is making her debut today. Its not late, its your time- I knew it would be today. Nothing spectacular is happening today in the secular world, but here in heaven we are celebrating your acceptance of My love and boldness to walk in it unhindered and unafraid to reveal it to others. I love you and know I Am with you wherever you go; I AM with your words and in your heart. Be brave. I AM."

"Good morning-How is your faith today? Are you doing better knowing I Am near?"

"Now we are going to go deeper still. In this place there are many hidden treasures; some that take time to excavate. When you hear Me, don't question My Words just ask for My strength and go deeper. Is it hard or scary? This place requires a new level of trust-without understanding. Do you trust Me enough to move without knowing why I AM asking you to move? You must trust that I Am love and that I only have great plans for you before we proceed."

Its hard because I fool myself into thinking I am in charge. You give me free will and I come to your desk/office for help then go back out into the world with the memory of what you said. Instead of walking beside you in strength in confidence-help me Lord. I don't want memories of your strength – I want it now Lord- where we are side by side wherever we go.

"Close your eyes, take My hand. I have always been here, you haven't known it but I AM with you. The truth is that you only seek Me when you need Me. Friends are closer than that, they speak to each other and don't act like the other is there for advice or help and you don't talk to them about other things. You have known Me for a while. I know your wants, desires and struggles even before you ask, so let's talk about other things too-lets impart My love on other people. Ask for intercession for those who don't know Me or those who have run from Me. Just because you are not asking for your need to be met or protection from the enemy doesn't mean I won't already have it covered. Trust that I love you-period. Trust that we can go beyond your struggles and move into this lost world I call the wilderness. They need Me because they don't have Holy Spirit inside of them and are drowning in sin. Some are even fooled to think there's another way to My Father. I AM the ONLY Way. Some worship false idols including themselves-they think they have all that they need and think that I Am a myth and a false hope-for fools. I can intercede, but they need you to pray. Instead of being afraid-use your wings and pray for your enemies and the lost, I will protect you from the enemy."

"Draw near to Me now. It is beautiful in this place. The colors of Zion radiate from Me. Although I glimmer, your eyes cannot behold My splendor. For now you can only encounter a portion of My glory- your eyes cannot handle My glory. In heaven- your new eyes can behold My splendor because you won't have things of this world keeping you from Me. For now what you can have is My peace, joy, love and never ending devotion to you. Once you accepted Me as Lord and Savior I have never left your side. Be of good cheer- I know things seem the same as every other day but this day is unique. You have allowed Me into your secret place where you keep your deepest fears, things people don't know about you and even the place you store all your regrets. Imagine a house, we are walking room by room and discussing what you keep there. Down the hallway to the right you keep your insecurities- you keep them close at hand because you feel comfortable and think these weaknesses and fears are who you are. We are going into this room and are going to take them out one by one and escort them out of your house.

-Fear of rejection is sitting at your desk in this room. It rules your life by keeping you held back. Its time has come and is no longer of any use. With My breath, I remove this from this place. Next, sitting at your make up mirror is pride. When you reject yourself and feel bad about yourself, you grab pride to come and defend your honor. Pride is not your friend- it's built upon your strength and not Mine. Pride looks like it's a defender of who you are; actually it's taking My place and is not welcome here. Your pride is fighting Me telling you that if you don't take pride in yourself others will take advantage of you. That's a false hope and a lie. Do you trust that I AM for you? Then give Me your pride and it will be replaced with My strength.

-Insecurity is hiding under the bed. It reaches out and tries to trip you in your life-its too scared to come out and only causes you to stumble. Lets kneel down together and pull out insecurity. Tell her its time to go. Release her now- out of this place. This room filled with insecurity, pride and fear of failure is now a peaceful place filled with sunshine and warmth. Lots of windows and a view of the ocean from the mountains. It's a place where there are no doors closing it off because they're no longer anything to hide and protect. There's a comfortable chair and a great big pillow. Sit and be still in this place. This is My refuge for you. Its light radiates in a comforting level. It brings you joy from the inside out because there's nothing to be afraid of or feel like you have to defend. Your flesh will expect to be able to find fear of rejection, pride and

insecurity, but they have all vanished by My love. When this world pressures you and you are running down this hall looking for your old "friends" who you thought were your safeguard and protection, you will only see My light radiating from this place into the hallway and will be comforted knowing that <u>truth</u> has taken its place. My love is perfect and is enough for you and all you need is this room because I AM here. Your refuge is found in Me alone. There are other rooms farther down the hallway.

-Ambition, destinations and lastly the place you store your treasures. Ambition is great and gives you a sense of purpose. We are going to invite ambition to join us back in the refuge room. Outside of My shelter ambition is not of Me. Once it comes under My authority and rule in this place its now a wall of books- it has a different look to it in this room. Its no longer out for gain- It's out for expanding My Kingdom-My Father's love for the lost. It no longer is allowed to fill you with anxiety or worry because of all these resources on this shelf have already been given to you. You only need to ask if it's the right time and for the right person- is this what I need right now? If I tell you not now, be ok to put that back on the shelf and save it until My works have been made ready for that resource to be used.

-Destination seems like it's an unattainable place because you are searching for something that is always changing. Destinations perspective changes once you arrive. It tricks you into feeling let down or even sad this location or circumstance is not your normal residence or seems too impossible to get to. Lets go outside and release destination. It's a lie that no longer keeps your feet bound and pulled in all directions. Destination is also back in this first room. I have called you to Be Still and know that I Am God. In My dwelling place and in My refuge is where you belong. That's the only place you are called to be. If you rest in this place of My strength and trust in My resources and My timing, I will take you to physical places, but you won't go there upset its not your permanent home-feeling regret or fear that you can't stay. When you go you will just be in the moment and be able to love those I have called you to serve in this place. When you love there will be no regrets because We go together. There's only one place to go now-this room on the right. I Am your treasure, because you treasure Me and My will for your life this room has a beautiful back door that leads out. We can go anywhere together from here. Before you go out –ask Me to guide you where and when before you go to the door to ask, take time to feel My warmth and peace in this place.

105

All things you do, your job, your role as mother, friend, student, sister, and aunt should come form this place. A place of knowing your value in My eyes- a place that no longer fears this world and the lies that fill it. A place that is no longer intimidated by earthly circumstances. When people come at you, those that used to make you reach for pride and insecurity, picture them at the bottom of this cliff and they are throwing pebbles as us sitting outside on the porch together enjoying My creation. Would that intimidate you?"

"Man has no strength over you anymore. Respect and honor the authority you have been placed under but don't fear it or let yourself feel inferior ever again. Mere pebbles from a distance is their only true power- nothing that could ever shake you from this place where I dwell. When we go out together we will find all kinds of people along this path. Some will reject us, but that's ok, remember their power never impacts My strength and My refuge. There's also a great multitude that will be glad they found Me through you. Holy Spirit welcomes them into their place with Me. You no longer feel compelled through gain, ambition or distraction, you are just walking with Me welcoming anyone to join us along the way. It's not a competition for My attention when they join us- its just family. You are all sons and daughters when you seek My love. This path is not difficult or scary; its full of love and laughter because the fight has already been won and nothing can shake My place in your heart anymore. The lies that kept you from Me in this place are gone and now it's just us together- Love."

"When things don't seem like they are going your way, look around. It just might be that they are not what you are used to fighting for. Maybe its something not worth fighting for anymore-its not the battle I want you in. I AM not saying to divorce someone- I Am referring to work and friendships. Why are you fighting to push the stone up the hill when the hill has a point to it and cannot hold the stone so it will just roll back down the other side? The other side feels as though you have accomplished the goal, but the effort is fleeting because the stone rolls far away and is no long in anyone's sight to care about your efforts. This is called striving. Striving is not of Me. I AM resting in the valley where its peaceful because I know My Father has already won and He will provide for all My needs. Come sit here with Me in the green grass and just enjoy the view. The mountains are beautiful here and they require no work to enjoy them. I made them for you to enjoy. They were made by My voice. Don't make your life harder than it needs to be in an effort to feel needed. When you are seeking man's approval by your hard work and efforts this is striving and We do not want that in your life. Are you ready to rest in the valley and relax- knowing you don't have to strive to achieve so all your needs will be met? Do you trust Me? Then lets walk from this mountain base where rocks have scratched and bruised you for so long in your efforts to "achieve" success. Lay your stone down and take My hand. Most people have fallen for this lie because they don't see what We see- that its wasted effort and time no matter where you get to on the mountain or no matter how many rocks you manage to push over the top. The top is a place of pride because you have elevated yourself by your works. My Father's Words and love for you are all you need. The work was finished on the cross, so lets rest in the peace that offers."

Ok so now that we are sitting in this peaceful meadow together- its beautiful and peaceful, but I still have to work in life. How can I work to earn wages sitting in a meadow?

"The meadow is a state of mind. In this meadow state of mind you are at peace in your Father's love. You are not fighting to gain traction or even fighting to not get trampled on. If someone is difficult to deal with, you will be in a much better place to give them empathy and truly listen. The goals and expectations set before you are fine, but don't build a mountain in this valley to demonstrate your worth. It looks ridiculous to see a man made hill in this place: you forcing rocks up and over this hill because its obvious you are only wanting to be noticed. Like a child that says, "Look at me." Others who are not the parent only have sarcasm in their

107

encouragement because they knew you created the entire circumstance and they can see through it."

So how do I move up and peruse my goals without making myself look silly and make it harder than it actually is?

"Stop calling everyone to stop what they are doing to watch you. We see you and We will provide all your needs if you seek Our will for your life. Hard work is noble to earn wages, but exhausting yourself and creating man-made mountains was never in your job description. Work and be successful, but if you don't accomplish everything you wanted to accomplish that day, lay it down- the good news about the valley —the rocks will be right where you left them. This is what's different-its flat and unlike the mountain —you don't have to fight to keep the position on the hill. When you accomplish the goal-I see it-don't get out the trumpets and call everyone around to see your victory- that's pride rising up. I promise that I will call all these successes to their minds when the time is right for promotion and review. Be nice to those I have placed around you-teach them the peace of My Father's love in this place. When your workload has been made easier- rejoice and don't feel as though something's wrong and that you are not needed. Its just Me giving you time to rest and to be with Me. Remember, you have left that mountain called striving and are here with Me. Lets enjoy the view and help call others to this place of peace and love. Some may become combative and try to fool you into picking up the rocks and walking back toward the mountain. But the mountain is not where My love is. Stay here."

"Daughter I love, don't be afraid. I know sometimes you feel insignificant and even forgotten. You are not alone and you are not forgotten. I AM with you always. Tune out the thoughts that are not of Me-those that make you fight unnecessarily for your fame. These are man made mountains I warned you about. Put down the rocks and just sit with Me-I'll handle the rest. I have plans for you, in your waiting, don't go around trying to find significance- I have called you Mine-Is that not significant enough? I know its hard when you see others gaining attention, their lives seem so effortless while you exhaust yourself and feel far less important no matter what you achieve. That's because you are doing works of the flesh and not what I have called you to do. Do you remember? I have called you to love My people-all people-no matter what they believe in- I have not forgotten them. I AM calling them to Me too. Do you trust Me?
"Do you really trust Me?" "Then stop competing and trying to prove your worth. Imagine two girls on a swing- one is swinging gently with a smile on her face, enjoying that she's getting to swing- she's doing the work to keep the motion going but its not exhausting her. The other girl has a tight grip on the rope and stern look on her face and she's pumping as hard as she can so she can be better. Is the girl pumping and straining to achieve such great heights better? How does she look from the outsider's perspective?

Weird- like she's competing for her mother's attention.

"Do you think the girl gently swinging or the girl going high with an eager and forceful look on her face is more approachable?
Do you believe I will provide for them both equally? Why doesn't the gentle girl fear for things she wants in life? She has put her trust in My efforts not hers. The few extra rocks you might push over the mountain in your own efforts or the maximum height you achieve on the swing is not worth missing out on My calling for your life. Lets slow the swing down, down to a stand still. Now stop the swing. Do you trust Me?
Let Me push you. The same peaceful beat your wings provide is the pace at which your swing should be going. I AM not out of My own timing and if you are allowing Me to control your pace in this life you will be filled with My joy and peace."

What about when I feel like I'm being forgotten or not being able to do the things I feel like you want me to do? Everyone else seems to be doing what they want to do and gaining all the glory and attention.

"Is that what you want, glory? That's idolatry and I know you really don't want that. Really the problem is you feel insignificant; that I have forgotten you or that you feel like you have nothing to offer this world-that's a lie from the enemy-shut him down." Forgive me Lord for believing the lie.

"You are not in competition with each other so put down your fighting gear. You are in a war against the enemy and if you get jealous of others instead of being truly happy for them you are allowing the enemy to gain traction. What other people do, no matter what notoriety they gain-does not change who you are in My eyes or My plans for you. You will do great things in My Name but you have to be at a place of rest that I have told you about- not at a place of insecurity, competition and battle for attention. I see you so you don't need to pump and get your swing up so high to prove you are valuable enough to be used by Me too. Then why wait?"

It doesn't seem fair- they swing so effortlessly with a happy look on their face –it doesn't even seem like they are even trying.

"That's because they aren't. Those that love Me allow Me to push them so they don't fear their worth and they don't use their strength –they use Mine. Others in the world that don't know Me and have that "look" are just content with what they are doing and don't feel like more effort is necessary."

So, you made me with a determined spirit to go out and fight, to be better and constantly look to see what can be better and now I am supposed to be content sitting gently on a swing? It doesn't seem to fit who you made me to be-I don't want to be jealous of those around me but I also don't want to feel like its so slow and boring- I want to fight for your Kingdom and it seems like something's missing.

110

"The swing is only where your mind's <u>pace</u> needs to be. I have not called you to literally sit on a swing-but to go there in your mind and check which position you are in: the girl I'm able to gently push or the girl fighting to go higher in your own strength. The desires of your heart will be fulfilled but you have to remove the things that keep Me from fulfilling them. Your own ambition for fame and worth is #1. I know this comes innocently because you feel overlooked and just want to be valued-but it's the enemy making you <u>think</u> you are unnoticed and not of value. People love and admire you- but the bigger point to remember is who you are in My eyes. #2 is your lack of faith in Me to use you. You think I'm not going to come through so if you want to do it-you better make it happen. Do you believe that I AM a good Father?" Yes Lord. *"Then trust Me for the desires of your heart. You trust Me for everything else- just not your dreams and things you truly want to be doing. Why do you think those desires are there? Relax. It is your calling."* It seems to good to be true.
"Is anything too difficult for Me? Why would I put something in your heart of hearts and not bring you to that place of fulfilling your dreams?"
I feel like I am going to miss it- it's why I'm anxious.
"My timing is perfect. Sit on the swing and let Me push you. When the enemy tries to make you feel forgotten and not worthy enough, know he's just trying to make you strive in your own effort and exhaust yourself-making you unable to be who I've called you to be and not be at a place where you can love those I have placed in your path."
"Our time together is very special to Me. I love that you miss Me when we are not alone together. I AM proud of the steps you have taken to grow in your faith and trust in Me. Things of this world will never satisfy you as deeply as truly knowing the depth of My love. I AM never too busy to hear you speak, I never take My eyes off of you so don't ever feel afraid or alone-I AM with you-rejoice in this place you have found Me. Do you know that I AM good and that I want what you want for your life? It may not be the timing to reveal and provide the things you desire right now and what you desire right now might only be because you are not brave enough to ask Me for what you really want in this life. Do you trust in Me? Do you believe I can provide you with the desires of your heart? Then sit on the swing and let Me push you gently. In this place of rest you glide effortlessly and there's no work to be done- there's no guilt in this place, no sense that you could be doing more or shouldn't be sitting in My place of rest with Me."

"When I push you on this swing it is a happy place of contentment because you feel secure knowing I AM in control. You know that you are where you are supposed to be and you don't compare yourself to anyone else there's no need to when we are together because nothing else matters. I love My daughter and I love her heart for the lost. I love her heart for My Word and her determination to not give up when things get tough. You entire life should move forward in this place- My strength, My love, My place of rest and complete utter happiness- It's My dwelling place. Let go of your anxieties, your worries and fears and just enjoy this time with Me. There is no greater accomplishment than complete surrender to My will for your life. It's not something that will be seen by all- it's a place of surrender and faith in I can do when you submit yourself to My will and not yours. Gently grab the ropes and relax- feel the gentle breeze and the sunshine on your face-knowing My eyes are fixed on you and everything is in My control; The Father who loves you."

"It's a new day- full of joy and My blessings. Rejoice and be glad. If you dwell on the things that are making you sad and feel unfulfilled you will be just that – sad and unfulfilled. Things will not always go your way- that doesn't mean you are out of My will or off the path I put you on.
Lets do something new. Lets read the pages My writers wrote for Us long ago for all ages. Although it was written for each generation that reads it- it is still not antiquated and historical-not relevant to you. My Words are timeless- if you don't search for Me in these pages you are missing out on who I AM."

"My son Solomon was blessed with wisdom and knowledge beyond understanding to most. He was blessed greatly with wealth as well although that was not what he asked from Me. Read **Ecclesiastes 1**.
This passage is not meant to depress or discourage you- its to hear and learn from the wisest man who will ever live on earth. His precepts are true. Things you toil over and strive for are fleeting and are like grasping at the wind- not full of substance- not what truly fulfills your calling- a relationship with Me is your calling and loving others into a relationship with Me is the work that I give you strength to do which is attainable because it is Us working through you and not by your efforts."

Ec.2 *"You skim over these verses and they are mere words on a page to you- someone else's' past- go back and read* **verses 4-9**. *Those things he acquired were great yet they are no big deal to those reading the pages about his accomplishments but yet you feel as though* things *and your efforts will leave some sort of legacy or lead to fulfillment."*

Read **vs. 10-11**. *"He rejoiced in all of his labor-he was unfulfilled because he wasn't rejoicing in Me. "There was no profit under the sun" because all you acquire, gain and build turns back to dust- there is no gain in earthly things. Open your ears to hear these words — don't live out the rest of your life to attain and achieve earthly titles or items."*

Vs. 12-16. *"Wisdom and knowledge is also a trap. They are great tools, but they are not the goal for your life. PhD's, Doctors and Theologians are not greater in My sight than you. I see your heart for Me and I see the love you have for those who have not yet found Me.*
I have given you the ability to learn, grow in knowledge and wisdom, but it becomes idolatry we you focus on you- it is Me in you who has granted you this ability to become knowledgeable so you need to acknowledge its not your works but Mine."

Vs. 17-26 *"Did you notice what he was doing wrong? Vs. 22. Striving. This is not of Me. Striving is fleshly gain which gets turned over to the next person in line- with no remembrance of what you did and no care of your items because now they are theirs."*

Ec. Chapter 3

*"You are better than mere animals- I put My breath in your nostrils and I set eternity in your heart. This is the longing that you feel- this is what drives people to "feel fulfilled." Fulfillment only comes through relationship with Us and trust in Me- not only for your salvation but for your joy. True joy is not from things, titles and accomplishments –joy is knowing who you are, your worth and that you don't have to do or gain anything in this life for Me to love you. I already do. Do you believe I Am the Son of God- Jesus? Do you believe I took on all your sins and died so that you may truly **live**? Then come to Me- I will give you rest. This resting place is on the swing we talked bout before. I will gently push you so you can feel My presence- knowing I AM always behind you and I never take My eyes off of you- you are My daughter whom I love. "*

Ok, so what do I do with my life? We grow up seeking things to obtain, places to go and titles to achieve wealth.

"Be still. TRUST in Me. Not your own efforts. Put everything you dream about in a pile- think about them one by one- lets pile them all together and hold nothing back- include your dream of dreams. Your knowledge and respect from man through a title only leads to envy."

Ec. 4 *"Fortune, fame and wealth are not what fill you with joy and peace. Solomon was explaining that anything apart from Me is vanity because there's no peace obtained by striving for it. One hand full is enough, be content in what you have and trust Me to provide you with the rest."*

Ec. 5 *"I have given you much, but the ruler of this world has caused man to be filled with greed. Always wanting more and never feeling like you are enough. It's a lie, filled with deception to steal the peace I have placed in your heart if you listen to him. You must learn to see through My eyes of what true worth and wealth is. Wealth and worth comes from The Father alone. Your worth was determined when I died for you. Not things you have stored away from your efforts. Can you put a price on eternity with Us? What if you gained the whole world's riches and worldly fame – would you trade that for a relationship with Me and eternity with Us?"*

"Then choose to see your wealth. Do you see the signet ring of The King that has been placed on your finger- making you daughter of The King? You are Mine, your dreams and desires are not foolish, but you need to give them to Me and walk in My love, not spending your time working to gain things for the second hand. The other hand is for holding Mine. This shows you are trusting Me to provide in the future just like I have for provided for you in the past."

Ec 6 *"Better is the sight of the eyes than the wandering of desire." "Ask to see the things I see. The hurting, the lost, the forgotten, the broken and the alone. Ask for courage and the words to speak life into them by sharing the Father's love. Desire is wandering because you will never be satisfied with what you obtain, if you seek earthly riches."*

Ec. 7 *"Who do you surround yourself with? Are people drawing you toward Me, or building you up for their gain? There is nothing of earthly works worthy to boast about. The One work of defeating death and sin was completed by My death and resurrection. Faith in this is all that's required, but yet fools spend their days on earth searching for security, something I have already provided them with. They seek earthly possessions, titles and provisions as though there's an ending place. A place where you can finally feel content and arrived at your destination. Wealth, fame, riches, titles all returns to dust because it was not created to endure. Only My love and The Father's love endures. You arrived when you accepted Me as Lord and Savior. Can you see through My Father's eyes at what has been given to you instead of the lens through the father of lies?*

Teach me Lord, what does that look like? We are taught we must go out, achieve and bring home success and wealth to provide for our needs and desires. How should I live?

"Be still in My dwelling place wherever I have called you. Calm and at peace doing whatever you love. Trust Me to provide and love My lost sheep who are in your pastures. When you seek the Kingdom of God instead of earthly riches, I will provide for you. Daily seek My face, seek to share The Father's love and His fame more than your fame. Give hope to the hopeless, love to the frightened, joy and peace to those who are fearful. There's nothing to fear when you trust in Me for everything. Do you trust in Me for <u>everything</u>? You can't say yes and leave some things hidden away from Me. I can't move forward with you any deeper until I have complete surrender. Do you trust me? Do you trust in who I AM? Do you trust I love you and will never leave you?"

"Search your heart. Ask for forgiveness for the sins that buried and forgotten. Now- look at your beautiful vessel. Your sins have been forgiven and removed. You must respect this beautiful vessel because it contains My Spirit. Protect your heart and mind, remembering you are My daughter, not the daughter of the father of lies who seeks to destroy you and My will for you. Your vessel is perfect; let My love fill your cup so that it overflows with My love, spreading to others who don't know Me. By mere association with you they will know that I AM here. All you do is love them, rest in My peace and strength, ask for words they need to hear and I will provide the rest."

Ec 8 " Your days here on this earth have already been determined. Do you want to toil to obtain things that will rust, rot decay and be eaten by moths or do you want to seek The Father's will for your days? Knowing The Father's will is easy- but you must want it more than the former earthly desires you once toiled over. Do you want your Father's will for your life or toil the rest of your days?"

"Then seek Me, take My hand and let's walk out into the deep- where you must rely on Me and Me alone. It will seem uncomfortable-even like you can't breathe at first but its not real-relax and trust. Push deeper and see you can do the impossible with God's strength. Are you willing to do what We ask of you even when your flesh wants to cry out in fear, weakness or even anger? When these feelings come up, ask for forgiveness because this is revealing your weakness in your faith."

118

Ec. 9 *"Many people get off path because they don't take time to be still and listen to My voice. They are frightened because they are letting circumstances control their value and determine their future. But you are wise because you have sought Me and My wisdom and have chosen not to toil for earthly gain. Rejoice- you are among the very few- truly wise."*

Ec10 *"Now that your vessel has been cleaned and you are seeking your Father's will for your life, take heed. Know that many are drawn to your because they see Me in you. Guard your word and your actions; protect My Father's Name."*

Ec. 11 *"Give out of the abundance of which I have already given you, trusting that you will lack for nothing."*

Ec. 12 *"There will be a time when all comes to an end. There is a time for you now in this place. You have not missed the calling upon your life. There is so much for you to do if you are willing. The only work that can be done that is not vanity is done in My Name and for the Father's Glory. You are a beautiful daughter with many blessings yet to be revealed. Seek Me daily, trust in My strength and My love for you."* Abba.